GUIDE TO THE
McCORMICK COLLECTION

GUIDE TO THE
McCORMICK
COLLECTION

of The State Historical Society of Wisconsin

Edited by Margaret R. Hafstad

MADISON
STATE HISTORICAL SOCIETY OF WISCONSIN
1973

Copyright © 1973

THE STATE HISTORICAL SOCIETY OF WISCONSIN

Manufactured by Worzalla Publishing Co., Stevens Point, Wisconsin

---

1. McCormick, Cyrus Hall, 1809–1884 — Archives.

2. McCormick family—Archives. I. Hafstad, Margaret R., ed. II. Title.

HD9486.U4M38   016.681'763   73-1216

ISBN 0-87020-124-7

PREFACE

THE MCCORMICK COLLECTION, as its name implies, is a collection of papers—of individuals, companies, and organizations—based on but not limited to the life and work of Cyrus Hall McCormick, inventor of the reaper. Following his death in 1884, McCormick's widow and children began employing secretaries to seek out and preserve manuscripts and memorabilia relating to the inventor and the development of the agricultural implement industry. From that time to the present, subsequent curators have assembled and organized a mass of material consisting of more than two million unbound manuscripts, almost three thousand volumes, and a large quantity of non-manuscript items such as photographs, books, publications of the McCormick companies, agricultural machinery and models, and museum pieces.

By 1919, the family-supported McCormick Historical Association had outgrown its quarters in the McCormick mansion at 675 Rush Street in Chicago. It was then moved to the large stone carriage house at the rear of the property, where extensive remodeling provided a library, museum, offices, and facilities for research. When the land and buildings were sold in an estate settlement in 1949, the holdings were placed in storage until 1951, at which time Anita McCormick Blaine, after having had her representatives investigate as many as thirty repositories, presented the complete collection to the State Historical Society of Wisconsin. Here, at this Midwestern location, Mrs. Blaine concluded that the outstanding American history library of the Society, and the reputation of the University of Wisconsin as a liberal arts and agricultural institution, would assure maximum use of the Collection by researchers.

The McCormick Collection of 1951 was composed of the papers of Cyrus Hall McCormick; domestic and foreign correspondence and business papers of the various McCormick companies in Chicago prior to 1902; and a number of collateral collections relating to agriculture and particularly to McCormick's native state of Virginia, including the papers of James D. Davidson and James McDowell of Rockbridge County, Virginia. However, since the arrival of the original Collection at the Society, it has been augmented greatly by the addition of other papers, many of them paralleling the inventor's manuscripts but most of them widening the fields of interest and sources for research. It was not typical of the McCormicks to remain idle or to discard evidence of either their personal or their public activities.

The papers of Nettie Fowler McCormick, the inventor's widow, were presented to the Society in 1953 and 1956 by the Nettie Fowler McCormick Biographical Association, along with the papers of her daughter, Mary Virginia McCormick. Shortly thereafter correspondence and reports relating to her son, Stanley R. McCormick, were received; and in 1958 the papers of another son, Harold F. McCormick, were presented by Harold's son, Fowler McCormick. In 1958 also, most of the papers of Anita McCormick Blaine were presented by Mrs. Blaine's granddaughter, Anne (Nancy) Blaine Harrison, and were completed with additions sent by Mrs. Harrison in 1971. In 1960, the papers of Cyrus H. McCormick, Jr., including much material on the McCormick companies and the International Harvester Company, were given by his son, Gordon; and additions were received from Gordon McCormick's estate in 1968.

In 1959 the International Harvester Company shipped several truckloads of farm implements and models to Stonefield, the Society's farm and craft museum at Cassville; and when the old McCormick Works at Chicago was closed, nineteen tons of financial ledgers were sent to the Society, all relating to the McCormick companies, other parent companies of the International Harvester Company, and International Harvester itself. Following the death in 1955 of the co-ordinator of the McCormick Collection, Herbert A. Kellar, his papers were added, including

those of Everett E. Edwards and Solon Robinson, used by
Kellar in his own research. Other, smaller groups of papers
have been received at various times since 1951, such as those of
William Steele McCormick in 1953.

Due to its size and complexity, and despite several segments
that overlap in time and content, the Collection covers a wide
range of subjects. The papers deal extensively with McCormick
family affairs and the McCormick companies; with the development and spread of the agricultural implement industry in the
United States and abroad; and with many phases of rural life
and agriculture, particularly prices and production. The growing
wealth of the McCormicks, and their desire to be of influence,
created manuscripts relating to railroad, timber, and mining investments; Democratic party politics of the nineteenth century;
Presbyterian church history and missions; educational institutions; wide-ranging philanthropies; and Chicago social and economic life. The Virginia Papers, assembled to serve as a background to the inventor's association with the state where he
first developed the reaper, provide information on local commerce and business, early iron furnaces, agriculture in the Valley
of Virginia, state and local politics, slavery and the Civil War,
canal construction, and land speculation.

Because the papers in this massive collection were acquired
over a long period, and processed by many different persons at
various times and places, consistency in arrangement has been
difficult, and detailed cataloging of all segments has been im-
possible. It is the purpose of this *Guide* to describe each group
of papers as a unit, pointing out the organization of each group
and mentioning any special finding aids. At this date a few personal papers are still restricted, and prospective researchers would
be advised to direct inquiries to the Manuscripts Curator at the
State Historical Society of Wisconsin before contemplating use
of the Collection.

A description of any collection of manuscripts such as this
always depends on the work of many archivists and curators who,
through the years, arranged and cataloged the papers and under-

took tasks that were long and tedious, often frustrating. I am fully cognizant of the contribution of those who preceded me. In the preparation of this *Guide to the McCormick Collection* I am particularly indebted to two of my former colleagues on the Society staff: to Josephine L. Harper, whose knowledge of the Collection and experience in writing guides was most helpful in discussing with me its form and content; and to Jack K. Jallings, who identified and described the hundreds of financial ledgers of the McCormick companies and the International Harvester Company. I further appreciate the care with which George West Diehl, genealogist and historian for the Rockbridge Historical Society, and Katherine G. Bushman, genealogist for the Augusta County Historical Society, provided supplementary facts and secured birth and death dates relating to The Virginia Papers. I have been aided in understanding the Collection by conversations with Lucile O'Connor Kellar, who served both the McCormicks and the Society as curator until 1963. Finally, the *Guide* could not have been written and published without arrangements made by Richard A. Erney, associate director of the State Historical Society of Wisconsin, and F. Gerald Ham, head of its Division of Archives and Manuscripts, and without funds provided by the McCormick Estates at Chicago.

MARGARET R. HAFSTAD

Madison, Wisconsin

CONTENTS

Eight pages of illustrations follow page 22

McCORMICK FAMILY PAPERS

1. McCORMICK, CYRUS HALL (1809–1884). PAPERS, 1788–1941. 212 boxes including 84 volumes, and 8 volumes.

Papers of Cyrus Hall McCormick, inventor of the reaper and Chicago industrialist, consisting of unbound correspondence and memoranda; letterbooks; legal records; volumes of accounts, receipts, check stubs, and inventories; and evidence compiled to support McCormick's claim to being sole inventor of the reaper. These concern the growth of the McCormick Harvesting Machine Company in both the domestic and foreign fields, and deal with McCormick's many interests, particularly his devotion to the Presbyterian church and to charities; his activities as a member of the state and national Democratic party; and his investments, chiefly in Chicago real estate, railroads, and mines. Although the inclusive dates range from 1788 to 1941, the bulk of the material appears within the life span of the inventor.

His Business

In 1831, C. H. McCormick built the first successful reaper at his father's forge in Rockbridge County, Virginia. Although he continued to make reapers and a hillside plow, in 1836 he and his father, Robert McCormick II, established an iron-manufacturing business at their Cotopaxi furnace in Augusta County, turning to their friend, William Massie, for financial assistance, and soon were operating as McCormick, Black & Co. When this failed five years later, the son directed all of his considerable energy toward improvement of his reaper and extension of

1

markets, traveling through New York state and the Ohio Valley region as far west as Missouri. While all of his first machines were built in his father's farm shop at "Walnut Grove," in 1845 he began licensing manufacturing rights to others, particularly in Cincinnati and Brockport, New York.

Letters of 1845 show his interest in the broad granary of the Midwest as the best field for expansion, and in the summer of 1847 he made arrangements to establish a factory in Chicago, first in partnership with Charles M. Gray, then with William B. Ogden and William E. Jones, and later with Orloff M. Dorman. Dissatisfied with the quality of reapers made by those whom he had licensed, and after disagreements with these early partners, he persuaded his brothers, Leander J. and William S. McCormick, to settle in Chicago and assist him in building an agricultural implement concern. By 1850 all manufacturing was being carried on by the Chicago plant of C. H. McCormick, with Leander J. in charge of production and William S. as manager of the office.

The three brothers aggressively created the world's leading producer of agricultural implements, operating under several titles for which pertinent correspondence and accounts appear in the papers. In 1859 all three shared in the firm under the name of C. H. McCormick & Bros.; in 1866, following the death of William S. the previous year, the name changed to C. H. McCormick & Bro.; and from 1874 to 1879 the company was known as C. H. and L. J. McCormick. With the entrance of Cyrus H. McCormick, Jr., into the firm in 1879, the McCormick Harvesting Machine Company came into being, operating as such until consolidation with the International Harvester Company group in 1902.

Throughout, Cyrus H. McCormick was the principal owner and driving force, but because he was so often absent from Chicago on business—he also lived in Europe from 1862 to 1864 and in New York from 1865 to 1871—voluminous correspondence was necessary. He communicated in great detail with William S. and the latter's successor, Charles A. Spring, Jr., each of whom wrote both McCormick and others concerning personal and business matters, patents, agreements, sales, agents, and investments. Leander's letters referred to design, operation, and patents. Other Company officials who carried on much correspondence were E. K. Butler, William J. Hanna, F. H. Mathews, James P. Whedon, and Leander's son, Robert Hall McCormick.

The inventor's papers demonstrate a genius in manufacturing and marketing that matched his ingenuity in building the first reaper. Depending on his brothers and others to carry on improvements in machines and expansion at the plant, he devoted himself to domestic distribution, the foreign markets, and never-ending battles with competitors over patent infringements. Manufacturing and sales correspondonce continued to originate in Chicago, while New York became his financial center and Washington the scene of his patent cases.

As early as 1845 he employed a cousin, John B. McCormick of Kentucky, as his first traveling agent, and there followed correspondence with many such agents throughout the Midwest and East, including James Campbell, R. T. Elkinton, Alexander M. Hamilton, and Thomas J. Paterson. A. D. Hager was sent to North Carolina in 1854 to introduce the reaper, and two years later to Illinois to observe demonstrations by competitors. Small-town implement dealers, and general agents such as H. C. Addis of Omaha and E. C. Beardsley of Minneapolis, came to be eyes, ears, and advocates for the sale of McCormick machines. Since sales of implements depended upon the success of agriculture, the country's economic and social conditions are consistently reflected in correspondence with both agents and farmers; references are made to conditions of crops, the influence of weather, crop yields, prices, advertising, problems of collection, competition, suggestions for improvement of machines, and occasionally, in the 1870's, to the Grange.

In 1848, following denial of McCormick's request for renewal of his original patent of 1834, there began litigation involving new applications, extensions, and infringements that lasted well beyond the inventor's lifetime. With improvements in the reaper and introduction of the mower, self rake, harvester, and binder, patent causes and manufacturing rivalries generated much of the correspondence. Included are letters and agreements relating to patentees and manufacturers such as John F. Appleby, Cornelius Aultman, William W. Burson, William Deering, Ralph Emerson, George Esterly, James F. Gordon, Marquis L. Gorham, Samuel Johnston, Sylvanus D. Locke, Henry F. Mann, John H. Manny, Charles W. Marsh, D. M. Osborne, J. Russell Parsons, George H. Rugg, Cyrenus Wheeler, Jr., Charles B. Withington, and Walter A. Wood.

To advise and represent him in business and legal matters McCormick corresponded with Paul Arnold, Henry Baldwin, Jr., William D. Baldwin, John R. Bennett, Roscoe Conkling, C. C. Copeland, Edward N. Dickerson, Cyrus Field, S. A. Goodwin, George Harding, Senator Benjamin Harrison, John N. Jewett, Reverdy Johnson, E. C. and W. C. Larned, William Lathrop, M. D. Leggett, and Peter H. Watson. Charles Colahan served as his traveling specialist, providing information from all parts of the country concerning competitors, patents, field trials, prices, sales, and even politics and investments.

In London in 1851 McCormick won the first of many medals at exhibitions in Europe; and thereafter, through many overseas trips and hundreds of communications, personally sought markets abroad. He employed foreign agents such as Otis S. Gage in England and James R. McDonald & Co. in Hamburg; in 1880 he sent George A. Freudenreich to Russia to develop agencies there. J. T. Griffin of the Chicago office sometimes represented him in Europe; the Confederate expatriate, Judah P. Benjamin, advised him on legal matters; and letters of the French economist, Michel Chevalier, discussed investments and politics with him.

The papers contain an assortment of legal manuscripts consisting of tax records, sales accounts, mortgages, leases, and some related legal correspondence. Interfiled in the unbound material are statements of assets, inventories, securities; a will of 1870; a history of the Company (1885); and a few items on the strike of 1885 at the McCormick Works. The volumes of accounts, check stubs, and receipts, all postdating 1862, cover chiefly records of household expenses, clothing, and travel.

His Church and Charities

Presbyterian church affairs were a dominant interest in the life of C. H. McCormick. Correspondence reflects growth of several Presbyterian churches in Chicago, church dissension prior to the Civil War, and controversies between conservative and radical theology. To advance his Old School point of view he endowed the Presbyterian Theological Seminary of the Northwest at Chicago, now called the McCormick Theological Seminary, fought to maintain conservative instruction, and contributed to its buildings and operation. One small volume contains a copy of the original endowments to the Seminary. He argued his beliefs through acquisition (1873) and publication of *The Interior* as an organ of Presbyterian conservatism, and carried on a large correspondence with churchmen such as Henry A. Boardman, Willis G. Craig, Ebenezer Erskine, William C. Gray, Leroy J. Halsey, Herrick Johnson, David X. Junkin, James McCosh, David C. Marquis, Francis L. Patton, William S. Plumer, Nathan L. Rice, Thomas H. Skinner, and Benjamin Mosby Smith. Allegations against Willis Lord appear in the papers, but there is no correspondence with him.

Other schools of which he particularly approved were recipients of McCormick's support. He gave to the endowment for Washington College in Lexington, Virginia, now Washington and Lee University; he corresponded with its president, Robert E. Lee, and with trustees John W. Brockenbrough, Bolivar Christian, and Robert D. Lilley. Among other institutions he aided were Union Theological Seminary in Virginia, John A. McAfee's Park College in Missouri, Virginia Military Institute, the University of Virginia, Hastings College in Nebraska, and Lake Forest University at Chicago.

McCormick corresponded with and supported the evangelism of Dwight L. Moody, and established a family tradition of consistent aid to the Young Men's Christian Association. Appeals for financial assistance, always common, increased following the Civil War when a flood of pleas from Virginia and other parts of the South came to McCormick. He selectively responded to numerous individuals; and letters, accounts, and check stubs reveal his concern for impoverished churches and the welfare of Negroes, with substantial contributions especially to the Southern Aid Society.

His Politics

In politics McCormick was a Democrat, taking an active though somewhat sporadic interest in national conventions and election compaigns. Being opposed to both abolition and secession, his correspondence prior to the Civil War emphasizes his hope that both his party and his church could help to prevent a break between the states. In 1860 he wrote E. W. McComas concerning Stephen A. Douglas and the Democratic party's need for support from the South. For several months in 1860 and 1861 he published the *Daily Chicago Times* as a political voice— "I bo't the *Times* (Chicago) for opposition to the election of 'Old Abe' "—and *The Expositor* as a religious advocate of union.

In 1864 McCormick returned to Illinois from Europe to wage an unsuccessful campaign against John Wentworth as Democratic candidate for Congress, and except for that year and early in 1865 political correspondence in the period preceding 1871 is very rare. On November 12, 1864, the *New York World* printed a McCormick letter proposing ways to stop the war, and on December 19 McCormick wrote to President Lincoln suggesting that he be appointed as an emissary to Richmond to attempt a compromise settlement between the Union and the Confederacy.

Following the Great Fire of 1871, the family took up permanent residence in Chicago, and in 1872 and 1876 McCormick served as chairman of the Democratic state central committee in Illinois. Most of his political correspondence relates to this decade, and includes letters exchanged with B. F. Bergen, William Bross, Daniel Cameron, C. C. Copeland, Isaac R. Diller, W. T. Dowdall, Henry H. Finley, Melville W. Fuller, R. E.

Goodell, C. R. Griffing, Ozias M. Hatch, Thomas A. Hendricks, Abram S. Hewitt, Gustavus Koerner, John A. McClernand, Samuel M. Moore, J. A. Noonan, John M. Palmer, Augustus Schell, Horatio Seymour, the Democratic State Central Committee, and the Tilden and Hendricks Democratic Central Committee of Illinois. Correspondence with his friends James D. Davidson, Horace Greeley, Reverdy Johnson, Joseph Medill, Roger A. Pryor, and Samuel J. Tilden pertains to politics as well as to business and social matters.

His Investments

Letters, accounts, property lists, legal documents, bills, receipts, and check stubs all attest to McCormick's interest in a variety of investments. Account books are interspersed with entries showing speculations in railroads, mineral lands, and other properties, and one lists tenants and rentals for 1864–1865. Due to his long absences from Chicago, William advised and represented him in purchasing Chicago residential lots, negotiating mortgages and loans, and constructing offices and stores. Charles A. Spring, Jr., and A. C. Rogers were among the employees who wrote in his behalf regarding investments; his wife's brother, Eldridge M. Fowler, corresponded concerning lands, timber, and the reaper business; and a sister's husband and son, Hugh and Cyrus H. Adams, operated the Chicago commission house of McCormick, Adams & Co., later called C. H. McCormick & Co., frequently communicating with him.

Railroad and mine investments were handled through New York lawyers and financiers such as S. L. M. Barlow, James Buell, Henry Day, Daniel Lord, Jr., George Peabody and Co. and the latter's successor, J. S. Morgan and Co.; and he often sent C. C. Copeland to report on prospective investments. In his most successful railroad venture, the Union Pacific Railroad Company, and subsequent involvement with both the Crédit Mobilier and Crédit Foncier, he corresponded with Oliver Ames, George P. Bemis, Sidney Dillon, John A. Dix, John Duff, Thomas C. Durant, Henry S. McComb, and George Francis Train. Letters exchanged with McComb and with Edward Learned relate to the Southern Railroad Association and its railways, and to the Tehuantepec Inter-Ocean Railroad Co. projected across Central America. As early as 1866 an account book shows his interest in Iowa and Nebraska railroad construction through stock subscribed to the Iowa Railway Contracting Co., the Sioux City and Pacific Rail Road Company and the Cedar Rapids and Missouri Rail Road Company; and a decade later he was corresponding with John I. Blair, H. C. Parsons, C. E. Vail, John M. S. Williams, and Union Pacific associates concerning possible railroad extensions in Virginia and West Virginia.

The many letters and four volumes relating to mining and land interests document McCormick's least success in speculations. Investments in the Montana Mineral Land and Mining Co. and Arizona properties, and abortive attempts to obtain gold at the Dorn mine in South Carolina and silver at the Little Chief mine in Colorado, created much correspondence with Copeland, James S. Cothran, Sr., James S. Cothran, Jr., John V. Farwell, Robert M. Funkhouser, Jesse Hoyt, N. S. Keith, Thomas S. Morgan, Richard Remington, Silas M. Stilwell, and Henry A. Ward. Through John D. Imboden, John Letcher, and R. H. Maury he showed interest in assisting land development in his native Virginia.

In the 1870's the Mississippi Valley Society of London was formed to encourage European capital and immigrants to seek the Midwest. McCormick, who invested in it, headed the Chicago branch, retained its minutes book for 1873–1874, and corresponded with the Society, especially its manager of branches, C. R. Griffing. The inventor's foreign interests also included stock in the American Exchange in Europe, Ltd., and produced correspondence with its founders, Henry F. Gillig and Joseph R. Hawley.

His Family

Personal correspondence and accounts appear throughout Mc-Cormick's papers, becoming much more common after his mar-

riage to Nancy Maria (Nettie) Fowler in 1858. There are communications with his father prior to the latter's death in 1846,
with his brothers and sisters, and with other relatives and
friends, including his slave, Joe Anderson, whom he left in
Virginia. As his children grew, personal letters refer to family
and social life; and because he was so often absent from home,
reports on his houses and properties are common.

Early correspondence between Mr. and Mrs. McCormick appears but is limited, since she often accompanied him on his
trips. As she took increasing interest in her husbands affairs,
and their oldest son, Cyrus H., Jr., became active in the reaper
business, letters and telegrams among the three and with Company officers increased, particularly after 1878 when the inventor's health began to restrict his activities.

Following the death of Cyrus McCormick the papers concern
chiefly the trusts created by his will and the administration of
his estate (after 1890 referred to as McCormick Estates), including letters of Mrs. McCormick, and the new Company president,
Cyrus H., Jr., and his brothers, Harold F. and Stanley R., who
entered the Company with him. Some correspondence continues
concerning Leander J. and Robert Hall McCormick, whose interest in the Company the family bought out in 1890; and with
William Jenkins and John N. Jewett for the estate, and H. O.
Edmonds for the McCormick Theological Seminary. Letters
from individuals such as Edward A. Ackerman, who joined the
business after the founder's death, begin to appear. Many interviews and reminiscences concerning McCormick date from about
1900, some of them obtained by the McCormick Biographical
Association and some by Herbert A. Kellar, who became curator
of the papers in 1915.

Organization of the Papers

The Cyrus Hall McCormick papers are organized in eight
series. The first four, 1788–1941, composed of unbound manuscripts and letterbooks, overlap in dates, treat of the same subject matter, and contain chiefly correspondence and reports.

These are all cataloged, and include a number of letters copied from letterbooks of his companies. The legal documents of series five, *ca.* 1860–1890, are alphabetized but uncataloged. Series six and seven, 1848–1902, contain assorted receipts, business accounts, and record books, chiefly relating to family and household matters. Evidence to prove McCormick's claim to invention of the reaper is assembled in series eight, 1831–1931. Series six through eight are not cataloged.

2. McCORMICK, NETTIE FOWLER. (1835–1923). PAPERS, 1775–1949, 1962. 451 boxes including 49 volumes, and 1 package.

Papers of Nancy Maria (Nettie) Fowler McCormick, philanthropist and wife of the inventor, Cyrus Hall McCormick, including correspondence; legal documents; volumes of diaries, memoranda, and scrapbooks; and financial files. In addition, the papers contain letters, genealogies, recollections, and interviews relating to her collected by the Nettie Fowler McCormick Biographical Association; including the working papers of the association's secretary, Stella Virginia Roderick, who published a biography of Mrs. McCormick in 1956.

In their native state of New York, Nettie Fowler and her younger brother, Eldridge, became orphans at an early age and were reared by their grandmother, Maria Fowler, and an uncle, Eldridge G. Merick. By the age of twenty-one Nettie had completed public school, attended girls' seminaries for three years, taught a short while, and acquired a deeply religious character. While visiting in Chicago, she joined the Presbyterian church, and in 1858 married Cyrus Hall McCormick, already a successful industrialist in the production and marketing of agricultural implements.

Correspondence

By far the largest portion of Mrs. McCormick's papers is composed of correspondence, of three types: with family and friends; with officials of the McCormick Harvesting Machine Company and its successor, the International Harvester Company; and with individuals, organizations, and institutions involved in her many philanthropies. Her own letters consist of drafts made by Mrs. McCormick, copies filed by her secretary, Truman B. Gorton, and originals and typescripts obtained from recipients after her death. Interfiled are legal documents such as powers of attorney, indentures, and contracts; annual statements and reports; and a copy of her will (1910). Also included are six volumes containing copies of his mother's letters in the possession of Cyrus H., Jr., on which he penciled annotations.

Correspondence before her marriage consists chiefly of letters relating to her own and her husband's ancestors and friends. Throughout her adult life she was in contact with numerous relatives such as members of the Adams, Esselstyn, Fowler, McCormick, Merick, and Spicer families. Frequent separations from her children produced letters expressing her concern for them, and correspondence with those charged with their care. These continued when the children became adults, although Virginia's mental breakdown before she was twenty, and Stanley's breakdown about 1906, restricted their own correspondence. Anita, who as Mrs. Emmons Blaine became a philanthropist in her own right, corresponded regularly with her mother, as did Mrs. McCormick's sons, Cyrus H., Jr., and Harold and their families. In later years grandchildren, nieces, and nephews became correspondents, including especially grandsons Cyrus, Gordon, and Fowler McCormick, and nephews Arthur H. Fleming, Robert Hall McCormick, and William Grigsby McCormick.

Her children's marriages, as well as her own residence at various times in Chicago, New York, Washington, and Europe, brought her many friends with whom she corresponded. These included Mr. and Mrs. Henry Day, Mr. and Mrs. John V. Farwell, Mr. and Mrs. Marshall Field, Mr. and Mrs. Joseph Medill, Mrs. Potter Palmer, Elinor Medill Patterson, Mr. and Mrs. Roger A. Pryor, Mr. and Mrs. John D. Rockefeller, Sr., John D. Rockefeller, Jr., Mrs. Russell Sage, Charles A. Spring, Sr., Mr. and Mrs. Algernon S. Sullivan and Mary Price Walstrom; and, among her pastors, John Hall, Thomas C. Hall, and Nathan L. Rice.

The correspondence confirms a quality in Mrs. McCormick that her husband was quick to recognize—a keen sense of business judgment. She accompanied him on many trips, discussed problems and wrote letters for him, and in his absence received confidential and lengthy letters relating to his business and their family life. Having become completely conversant with the operation of the McCormick Harvesting Machine Company, she was well equipped to serve as her husband's aid and her eldest son's adviser when McCormick's vigor was reduced after his illness in Paris in 1878, and following his death in 1884. In 1878, for instance, in London she wrote the Lord Chancellor asking for an audience to discuss Company business; sent a letter to their European lawyer, Judah P. Benjamin; and wrote Cyrus H., Jr. at Princeton concerning business matters. A list dated 1884 details Company affairs with which she seems to have been particularly concerned that year.

After Cyrus H., Jr., entered the Company in 1879 and became president in 1884, frequent communications between son and mother discuss the business, the estate, and investments. She corresponded similarly with Anita and Harold; with her brother, Eldridge M. Fowler, who became vice-president in 1890, and with many Company officials. References are made to competitors, patents, and strikes of 1885 and 1886; the unsuccessful attempt to form the American Harvester Company in 1888–1890; and problems attending consolidation when the International Harvester Company was established in 1902. Her close contact with these interests, as well as investments and philanthropies, produced correspondence with lawyers, employees, financial agents, and advisers such as Edward A. Ackerman, Cyrus Hall Adams, Gertrude Beeks, Cyrus Bentley, Emmons Blaine, E. K. Butler, John A. Chapman, Charles Colahan, James S. Cothran, Jr., William, James, and Charles Deering, George Freudenreich, Isaac T. Gladden, J. J. Glessner, James F. and John H. Gordon, Mary Lathrop Goss, William J. Hanna, William Jenkins, John N. Jewett, Alexander Legge, J. Pierpont Morgan, D. M. Osborne, H. C. Parsons, George W. Perkins, Hiram B. Prentice, Charles

A. Spring, Jr., Frank A. Steuert, Judson F. Stone, George H. Sullivan, James P. Whedon, and John P. Wilson. To keep her informed, she received copies of many letters and reports from the McCormick Harvesting Machine Company and the International Harvester Company long after she ceased to be so closely involved.

In the 1890's, with operation of the Company under the firm guidance of her eldest son, Mrs. McCormick had both the time and means to give more attention to her absorbing interest in philanthropy, an interest that accounts for fully half of her correspondence. The McCormick Theological Seminary, her husband's original cause, continued to receive a major share of her attention and funds. Its administrators and faculty, as well as her own pastors at Fourth Presbyterian Church, consulted with her regularly and advised her on other schools and missions. Included is correspondence with men such as Willis G. Craig, Herrick Johnson, Cleland B. McAfee, James G. K. McClure, Sr., David C. Marquis, George Livingstone Robinson, Thomas H. Skinner, John Timothy Stone, and Andrew C. Zenos. Wives of many also wrote her, especially Mrs. Stone and Mrs. Zenos. Her correspondents among the Princeton faculty were James McCosh, Francis L. Patton, Henry Van Dyke, and Woodrow Wilson, whom she wrote even after Wilson became President.

Using the need for Christian service as her personal motivation, she became greatly interested in aiding small schools and academies, particularly those stressing self help for students, manual training, and domestic science. These were chiefly but not exclusively Presbyterian, and chiefly white although some were Negro. Letters give evidence of the extent to which she advised them, influenced their curricula, and helped to maintain them.

Among the many institutions she thus assisted were Blackburn College (Illinois), College of the Ozarks (Arkansas), Columbia Theological Seminary (South Carolina), Dubuque College and Seminary (Iowa), Greeneville and Tusculum College, later Tusculum (Tennessee), Hampton Normal and Agricultural Institute (Virginia), Harold McCormick School (Tennessee), Hastings College (Nebraska), Huron College (South Dakota), Jamestown College (North Dakota), Lake Forest University (Illinois), Macalester College (Minnesota), Morristown Normal and Industrial College (Tennessee), Park College (Missouri), S. P. Lees Collegiate Institute (Kentucky), Stanley McCormick School (North Carolina), State Agricultural and Mechanical College for Negroes (Alabama), Utica Normal Institute (Mississippi), Union Theological Seminary (Virginia), and Washington and Lee University (Virginia). Those with whom she corresponded included L. H. Blanton, William C. Clemens, S. A. Coile, R. B. Crone, Henry M. Gage, Charles Oliver Gray, Landon Carter Haynes, Judson S. Hill, Albert C. Holt, William H. Holtzclaw who wrote *The Black Man's Burden,* William M. Hudson, Leroy F. Jackson, Barend H. Kroeze, Hubert S. Lyle, John A. McAfee, Lowell Mason McAfee, S. J. McClanaghan, Bertha L. Roach McDonald, William S. Plumer, Benjamin Mosby Smith, Cornelius M. Steffens, and Warren H. Wilson. The extent of her personal involvement is illustrated by her many years of correspondence with Harold S. Clemons, the son of one of these men, whom she assisted through Massachusetts Institute of Technology.

Her interest in the welfare of those in the southern Appalachians led her to aid the Home Industrial School at Asheville under Florence Stephenson; and to give encouragement to the Laurel schools, and projects in mountain crafts, out of which grew correspondence with Frances L. Goodrich. She helped support Thornwell Orphanage in South Carolina, writing to William Plumer Jacobs; and she kept in touch with James G. K. McClure, Jr., of the Farmer's Federation in North Carolina.

Nearer home, Mrs. McCormick received requests from numerous civic causes in the Chicago area, and responded to many. For instance, she corresponded with Jane Addams of Hull House; Louise de Koven Bowen concerning the Juvenile Protective Association; Matilda B. Carse of the Women's Christian Temperance Union; Mary E. McDowell of the University of Chicago Settlement, whom she also sent as an emissary to the southern mountain schools; and Josephine E. Young of Rush Medical College's Orthogenic Clinic. Bible work and rescue missions were important to her, as is shown in correspondence with Norman B. Barr of Olivet Institute; Dwight L. Moody of the Chicago Evangelization Society and the Moody Bible Institute; and Emma Dryer, who was associated first with Moody and then with the Chicago Bible Society. Mrs. McCormick approved of the experimental Chicago Institute and received a few communications from John Dewey and Francis W. Parker. She regularly acknowledged requests from Arthur Burrage Farwell for aid to the Chicago Law and Order League, and from others in behalf of charities such as the Chicago Boys Club, the Beulah Home and Maternity Hospital, the Chicago Home for the Friendless, Pacific Garden Mission, and the Salvation Army. Louis H. Sullivan wrote her about plans she commissioned him to draw for the Presbyterian Hospital in Chicago, and for a girl's dormitory at Tusculum.

Letters concerning the Presbyterian church and its various boards of education and missions comprise much of the correspondence. Among the earliest are letters with Jane C. Hoge, Harriet S. Keep, Mary Brewster Laflin, Sara J. Rhea, and Lillias Horton Underwood, with whom she was associated on the Women's Presbyterian Board of Missions of the Northwest. She corresponded with Robert F. Sulzer, in charge of Christian education in Minnesota and North Dakota, and with the missionary Samuel A. Blair, whom she supported there. Harlan Page Cory interested her especially in home missions; and exchanges were numerous with Robert E. Speer, secretary of the Board of Foreign Missions for the Presbyterian Church in the U.S.A.

In her last thirty years, foreign mission schools claimed much of her attention; and both the personnel and the institutions were her correspondents as well as recipients of her largess. Among these were William N. Blair and Samuel A. Moffett at Pyeng Yang Station (Korea), C. K. Edmunds and Herbert E. House of Canton Christian College (China), Wilfred T. Grenfell and the Grenfell Association of America (Newfoundland),

Sam Higginbottom of Allahabad Christian College (India), Henry Winters Luce at Tengchow (China), Shantung Christian College (China), Robert S. McClenahan of Assiut College (Egypt), and John E. Williams of the University of Nanking (China). Letters from wives of many missionaries appear in the papers, and evidence of Mrs. McCormick's interest in their families is illustrated by two decades of correspondence with Luce's son, Henry R. Luce, the publisher, to whom she frequently gave advice on policy and the news.

The papers also document her great interest in both the Young Men's Christian Association and the Young Women's Christian Association—locally, nationally, and internationally. Through numerous letters exchanged with John R. Mott she aided the World's Student Christian Movement and the work of the International Committee of the YMCA. She corresponded also with Fletcher S. Brockman, George M. Day, Sherwood Eddy, Carlisle V. Hibbard, Richard C. Morse, and Luther D. Wishard concerning the YMCA; and with Grace Dodge and Elizabeth Wilson of the YWCA.

With her son, Cyrus H., Jr., she continued to publish *The Interior*, the Presbyterian church paper established by her husband, combining it in 1910 with an eastern journal, *The Westminster*, to form *The Continent*. Correspondence was carried on with editors William C. Gray, Everett Sisson, and Oliver R. Williamson.

Diaries, Memoranda, and Scrapbooks

The papers contain fourteen volumes of diaries kept by Mrs. McCormick, the first covering her three years in female seminaries in New York state, the next twelve including the period from 1856 through 1877, and the last recounting a trip to Egypt for Stanley's health in 1896. These have frequent gaps in time, from a few weeks to as much as three years, but entries are long and thoughtful, revealing much of the character of the woman who was Nettie Fowler McCormick. They demonstrate her desire to help others, her concern for her children, and the extent to which she served as counselor to her husband. Entries refer to discussions on plant expansion, her attitude toward mine investments, and her writing of business letters at McCormick's dictation. References are made to the Civil War, especially during its opening months while the family lived in Washington, and her later work with the New York ladies' Southern Relief Society.

In addition, there are two notebooks, 1852–1853, kept while Nettie was a student at Troy Female Academy in the state of New York; six very small books containing shopping lists and personal expenditures by Mrs. McCormick, especially while she was on trips abroad; and two volumes of diaries, 1851–1860, by her cousin, Ermina G. Merick, making frequent reference to Nettie.

Of the four volumes of scrapbooks, one records the success of the McCormick reaper at the London exhibition in 1862; one contains clippings of letters by McCormick published in church papers, 1868–1869, at the time of the Willis Lord controversy; and two consist of clippings, programs, and photographs, 1909–1912, regarding admission of Cyrus H. McCormick, Sr., to the Illinois Farmer's Hall of Fame.

Financial File

Mrs. McCormick's own habit of keeping lists, her use of cashiers and agents, and the complexity and size of her estate produced a large financial file. Miscellaneous records were kept prior to 1883, but thereafter they increased in detail and continuity. Unbound statements, five ledgers, and an account book list her donations between 1883 and 1923, including recipient, date, amount, and sometimes notation as to the purpose. Entries frequently overlap, but an alphabetical listing in the largest volume summarizes gifts totaling millions of dollars.

The files include two cash books showing expenditures for incidental items, 1884–1890; unbound statements relating to investments and net worth, 1892–1922; and real estate reports and cash statements, 1890–1923, for Mrs. McCormick and the trustees for her daughter, Mary Virginia. Financial accounts concerning stocks, taxes, and her properties and their upkeep are included, often with pertinent letters from agents such as John A. Chapman, Hiram B. Prentice, and Judson F. Stone. Domestic accounts, 1861–1923, are shown in a large file of bills, receipts, statements, and check stubs.

Six volumes of account books kept by personnel of the Stanley McCormick School from 1909 to 1918 complete the financial files. These record each student's payments for tuition, board and room, and cash or credit allowed for part-time work at the school.

Nettie Fowler McCormick Biographical Association

In 1932 three of Mrs. McCormick's children—Cyrus H., Jr., Anita, and Harold—formed an Association for the purpose of having their mother's papers arranged, acquiring letters others had received from her, and obtaining interviews and recollections from persons who had known her. Virginia Roderick was employed as secretary, and served in this capacity until 1956 when the work of the Association was completed and her biography, *Nettie Fowler McCormick,* was published.

The Association's papers are composed of Miss Roderick's correspondence with individuals, organizations, and institutions in the search for letters and information; recollections and interviews she obtained from hundreds of persons who had known Mrs. McCormick; and both original and copied letters relating to Mrs. McCormick, some of which Harold originally had in his files. Included also are copies of letters from Eldridge M. Fowler to Cyrus H., Jr. concerning Mrs. McCormick, and letters and notes that James G. K. McClure, Sr., had collected for a memoir of Mrs. McCormick.

In addition, there are copies of manuscripts and correspondence loaned by members of the Fowler, Spicer, Merick, and McCormick families, including Fowler family business papers dating back to 1802. Much genealogical and biographical information is filed, as are many clippings. Miss Roderick's own notes, memoranda, reports, working papers, and manuscript for her book are included.

Organization of the Papers

The Nettie Fowler McCormick papers are organized in eight series. The first, 1843–1923, consists chiefly of letters sent; the next two, 1775–1939, are composed of correspondence and reports received. These first three series are cataloged. Series four, 1850–1912, consisting of diaries, memoranda, and scrapbooks, is uncataloged. Series five through seven, 1861–1923, make up the financial files, and none is cataloged. Series eight, 1802–1949, consists of manuscripts collected or created by the Nettie Fowler McCormick Biographical Association, and only the recollections and interviews are cataloged.

3. McCORMICK, CYRUS H., JR. (1859–1936). PAPERS, 1840–1942. 599 boxes including 268 volumes, and 8 volumes and 1 package.

Papers of Cyrus H. McCormick, Jr., Chicago industrialist, consisting of unbound correspondence and letterbooks; business records; and diaries, appointment books, school and personal health notebooks, scrapbooks, and memorial volumes of letters. These include papers concerning the two companies he headed; financial files relating to investments, real estate, and trusts; correspondence and reports regarding numerous committees, boards, organizations, and institutions to which he contributed both time and money; a large clipping file touching on all phases of his life; and manuscripts representing a multiplicity of family interests. Also included are papers of his first wife, Harriet Hammond McCormick, consisting of personal and social service correspondence, household records, and materials for her book on landscaping.

His Business Interests

Many segments of the papers concern the business life of Cyrus

H. McCormick, Jr., from the time he finished at Princeton University in 1879 until he retired from the board of the International Harvester Company in 1935. He became president of the McCormick Harvesting Machine Company in 1884 after the death of his father, Cyrus Hall McCormick, was made president of the International Harvester Company when it was formed, and in 1918 turned over that presidency to his brother, Harold, to become chairman of the board. The papers are composed of his private files from offices at his company, his home, and the McCormick Estates; they consist of correspondence, telegrams, memoranda of conferences, reports, agreements, appraisals, legal documents, and financial statements. Unbound papers and letterbooks contain correspondence with Company personnel, other business associates, and lawyers—all supplemented by his own diaries (1875–1930). Entries in the diaries were kept more faithfully in the earlier decades, and record contacts and comments often not found in letters. For example, Cyrus, Jr.'s detailed diary of disagreements and negotiations with his uncle and cousin, Leander J. and Robert Hall McCormick, appears for 1879, when the McCormick Harvesting Machine Company was agreed upon. His "traveling copy books" for 1881 to 1885 include the years he represented and counseled with his parents in learning the agricultural implement business.

The papers reflect steady expansion of the McCormick Harvesting Machine Company; the attempt in 1890 to combine with others in forming the American Harvester Company; successful consolidation in 1902 with McCormick's chief rival, the Deering Harvester Company, and three smaller concerns—the Milwaukee Harvester Company, the Plano Manufacturing Company, and the company of Warder, Bushnell, and Glessner—to form the International Harvester Company; the role of J. P. Morgan and Company in effecting consolidation; and problems attendant upon the government's subsequent anti-trust suit.

Internal operation, plant expansion, acquisition of factories producing materials needed by International Harvester, introduction of new lines of agricultural equipment, and both domestic and foreign marketing are revealed in communications passing through McCormick's offices. Letters received in 1886 from other manufacturers concern reaction to the strikes of that year, and later correspondence of the Company often makes reference to labor matters. Letters and reports appear from field agents suggesting improvements in machines; from factory personnel concerning production; and from the welfare department regarding working conditions, salaries, and pensions. Financial files include two volumes of notes on transactions and liquidation items relating to the McCormick Harvesting Machine Company and the Deering Harvester Company. Information gathered for his son Cyrus McCormick's book, *The Century of the Reaper* (1931), includes reminiscences of early International Harvester Company employees.

Frequent trips in the United States and Europe by McCormick and his brothers, Harold, and for a few years, Stanley, produced numerous messages on behalf of their Company, an organization that came to own plants in cities other than the Chicago area and had production agreements with many foreign manufacturers. To maintain such an enterprise and handle their other investments, voluminous correspondence was carried on with other Company officials, bankers, lawyers, and competitors, chief of whom were Edward A. Ackerman, Cyrus H. Adams, Edgar A. Bancroft, Gertrude Beeks, Cyrus Bentley, E. K. Butler, John A. Chapman, C. C. Copeland, James S. Cothran, Jr., W. V. Couchman, Paul D. Cravath, Charles and James Deering, John V. Farwell, John C. Fetzer, Eldridge M. Fowler, C. S. Funk, J. J. Glessner, William J. Hanna, John Hays Hammond, John R. Hoagland, James L. Houghteling, William Jenkins, William H. Jones, H. H. Kohlsaat, Preston B. Clark, Alexander Legge, George W. Perkins, Herbert F. Perkins, Hiram B. Prentice, George A. Ranney, W. M. Reay, John D. Rockefeller, Jr., Charles A. Spring, Jr., Frank A. Steuert, Judson F. Stone, George H. Sullivan, H. B. Utley, and John P. Wilson.

In addition to the business of his companies, McCormick's papers contain correspondence, reports, stock purchases, and negotiations concerning a great number and variety of investments typical of an American capitalist. Secretaries kept him informed of his financial situation, and provided him with many reports and letters of background information and advice. The diversity of such materials is illustrated by files for McCormick Estates through which the family maintained a large interest in Chicago real estate, including the Reaper Block and the Chicago Stock Exchange Building; the Merchants Loan & Trust Company and the Chicago and Northwestern Railway Company, of which McCormick was a director; the Calumet Canal and Dock Company at Chicago; the Bunker Hill and Sullivan Mining and Concentrating Company of San Francisco, through which McCormick invested in mines of the West and Canada; the Beaver Cove Lumber and Pulp Company, Ltd., later the Canadian Forest Products Company; and the Deepwater Coal and Iron Corporation operating in Alabama, West Virginia, and Kentucky. His interest in Elm Farm, and at his country estate, "Walden," at Lake Forest, led him to join with a small group in 1913 to form the Lake Forest Improvement Trustees, for the purpose of purchasing and developing property in that Chicago suburb.

His Public Service and Philanthropies

Correspondence, reports, and dockets for contributions to charities constitute a large portion of the papers, representing hundreds of appeals and giving evidence of selective response by Mr. and Mrs. McCormick. Through the so-called Family Gift Syndicate, they co-operated with other members of the family in giving aid to relatives in financial need; and they assisted many friends directly. Motivated by their daughter's interest in the missionary work of the Waldensian Society, for many years after her death they corresponded with and supported Luigi Angelini at a school operated by the society in Italy; but the chief beneficiary of their large Elizabeth McCormick Memorial Fund was child welfare in Chicago, especially open-air schools.

The Presbyterian church, locally and in the mission fields,

Cyrus Hall McCormick, *ca*. 1866.

Cyrus Hall McCormick and his wife Nettie
Fowler McCormick, pictured in 1884, the year
of the inventor's death.

Cyrus H. McCormick, Jr., Anita McCormick Blaine, and Nettie Fowler McCormick, *ca.* 1905.

Nettie Fowler McCormick at the International Exposition, Paris, 1900.

John D. Rockefeller (left), his wife (seated at center), and Nettie Fowler McCormick (seated, right). The children seated in front are Harold F. McCormick, Jr., and his sister Muriel.

Harold F. McCormick with his children at "Walnut Grove," Rockbridge County, Virginia, 1922.

Family gathering at the northwestern Wisconsin camp of Dr. William C. Gray, editor of *The Interior,* summer, 1888. (Standing, left to right) Ned Ryerson, Cyrus H. McCormick, Jr., Dr. Gray, Stanley R. McCormick. (Seated on chairs) Harold F. McCormick, Nettie Fowler McCormick, Mary Roberts. (Seated on ground) Anita McCormick, John Ryerson.

McCormick Works of the International Harvester Company, Chicago, 1947.

Emmons Blaine, Jr., with Nettie Fowler
McCormick and Anita McCormick Blaine, *ca.*
1892.

Harold F. McCormick and his wife Edith
Rockefeller.

A McCormick reaper at work in a Wisconsin
grain field.

Nettie Fowler McCormick and her son Stanley,
ca. 1900.

consistently received communications and funds. Until 1910 McCormick assisted his mother in supporting publication of *The Interior,* and for a few years had a financial interest in *The Continent.* From the time of his father's death to his own, he showed great concern for the McCormick Theological Seminary, of which he was a trustee and treasurer and for which his papers contain much correspondence concerning faculty, buildings, minutes of meetings, and treasurer's reports.

In 1889 he became a trustee for Princeton University, and for the remainder of his life corresponded with faculty members and other trustees, adding to his papers both manuscripts and printed reports concerning the University and its committees. To a lesser extent his papers contain letters and reports relating to Lake Forest University, of which he was a trustee, and to other schools such as Dubuque Theological Seminary (Iowa), Hampton Normal and Agricultural Institute (Virginia), Macalester College (Minnesota), and Washington and Lee University (Virginia). Institutions in and near Chicago, such as the Allendale Farm for boys, Olivet Institute, and Presbyterian Hospital, also received his attention.

The work of the Young Men's Christian Association was of particular interest to McCormick, and there is ample evidence that he served as a working member of the Chicago YMCA and the board of the International Committee. Correspondence of 1919 includes the weeks he spent in France and England assisting the YMCA in its relations with soldiers. The papers also demonstrate the McCormicks' interest in the Young Women's Christian Association and the Visiting Nurse Association of Chicago.

In 1917, his service as a member of the government's Special Diplomatic Mission to Russia (the Root Commission) produced letters, reports, and clippings concerning post-revolutionary economic and social conditions there, including progress of International Harvester Company agents in Russia. Financial records, and a few letters, demonstrate consistent contributions to the Democratic party; but very little evidence appears showing

direct political activity on his part, aside from his long friend-
ship with Woodrow Wilson. He did file a memorandum of a
conference with Robert Lansing in 1920, and received a long
letter concerning party finances in 1922 from Cordell Hull. On
March 16, 1935, he wrote his son, Cyrus, a confidential letter
concerning Franklin D. Roosevelt, and received an invitation to
call on the President shortly afterward.

McCormick was often asked to help welcome dignitaries to
Chicago, and committee plans for receiving men such as Admiral
George Dewey, Marshal Ferdinand Foch, Georges Clemenceau,
and David Lloyd George are filed with his papers. In the course of
his public service and the distribution of funds to charities, he fre-
quently referred to conferences in his diaries, and corresponded,
either directly or indirectly through secretaries, with many in-
dividuals. These included Robert Bridges, Fletcher S. Brockman,
I. E. Brown, Howard Crosby Butler, Willis G. Craig, Edward
P. Davis, John DeWitt, Sherwood Eddy, William C. Gray, A.
Woodruff Halsey, Sam Higginbottom, Herrick Johnson, Robert
S. McClenahan, James G. K. McClure, Sr., S. J. McPherson,
E. C. Mercer, L. Wilbur Messer, Richard C. Morse, John R.
Mott, Elihu Root, Everett Sisson, John Timothy Stone, Harriet
Taylor, Booker T. Washington, Woodrow Wilson, Luther D.
Wishard, and Andrew C. Zenos.

His Family and Personal Interests

The marriage of McCormick to Harriet Bradley Hammond
in 1889 brought into the family another whose personal interests and civic activities produced a volume of her own correspondence, memoranda, reports, clippings, and financial records.
These concern chiefly household matters; the preparation of
her book, *Landscape Art*; her community and social work in
Chicago; charities relating to memorials to her daughter; and
the Chicago YWCA building given in 1926 as a memorial to
Mrs. McCormick after her own death in 1921. Included among
the four financial ledgers is one listing her personal expenditures for charities.

The papers contain correspondence between McCormick and his wife, Harriet, and with their three children: Cyrus, who was first associated with the International Harvester Company in distribution and production then turned to writing; Elizabeth, who died at the age of twelve; and Gordon, who took up architecture. Much correspondence was carried on between McCormick and his mother, Nettie Fowler McCormick, or her secretary, Truman B. Gorton; between McCormick and his brothers, Harold and Stanley, and his sister, Anita McCormick Blaine; and between McCormick and Harold's son, Fowler, who became a Company official and in 1941 president of International Harvester.

Numerous letters to, from, and about members of the Adams, Esselstyn, Fowler, Hammond, McCormick, Merick, Shields, Spicer, and Stickney families are included. McCormick was involved in the administration of family estates and trusts for which many records appear in both his correspondence and business files. He administered the estates of his parents, and of his first wife, Harriet, and her aunt, Mrs. Elizabeth H. Stickney; was a trustee for the estates of his mentally incompetent sister, Mary Virginia, and brother, Stanley; advised his sister, Anita, on investments; and handled funds established in memory of his daughter and his wife. McCormick estates, investments, and obligations were so interlocking that periodic family conferences were held for which minutes were recorded, 1905–1932, and these are filed.

Very limited material appears relating to his second wife, Alice Marie Hoit, whom he married in 1927. Her correspondence concerning the YWCA is included, a few letters and clippings make reference to her, and she signed many letters for him while she was McCormick's secretary prior to their marriage.

Files kept by his personal librarian and private secretaries attest to McCormick's interest in art, music, rare books, and history. These are composed of correspondence, reports, articles, clippings, catalogs, and lists relating to diverse topics, among which are his art collection, archeological investigations at Sardis in Turkey, the evolution of the McCormick reaper, and information compiled by the McCormick Historical Association under Herbert A. Kellar. The McCormicks corresponded with the composer Serge Prokofiev, the pianist Gunnar Johansen, and the painter Vladimir Perfilieff; filed clippings concerning the Chicago Grand Opera; and gave active support to the Chicago Opera Association, the Art Institute, the Field Museum of Natural History, and the Chicago Historical Society. The papers also contain printed musical compositions by McCormick himself. Although he belonged to many local and national organizations, letters and accounts show him to have been particularly interested in the City Club of Chicago, the Commercial Club, and the National Civic Federation.

Involved as he was with city, national, and foreign interests, including relief to European countries following World War I, McCormick had contact with many noted persons who were not necessarily business associates. Consequently his papers contain communications, often brief and sometimes only social, with persons such as Philip D. Armour, Bernard M. Baruch, Jules Cambon, Albert H. Chatfield, Charles G. Dawes, Paul Deschanel, William E. Dodd, Cleveland H. Dodge, Baron Paul d'Estournelles de Constant, George W. Goethals, Charles Evans Hughes, Jean Jules Jusserand, Thomas Lipton, William G. McAdoo, Ignace Paderewski, Horace Plunkett, William A. (Billy) Sunday, Campbell Stuart, André Tardieu, and Henry Van Dyke.

Organization of the Papers

The Cyrus H. McCormick, Jr., papers are organized in twelve series, many of which overlap as to individuals and subject matter covered. The first three series, 1848–1936, are composed of unbound manuscripts and letterbooks containing correspondence, legal documents, reports, accounts, and clipping files handled by his business offices. Series one, containing chiefly correspondence, is essentially cataloged; series two, consisting of a subject file, is not cataloged; and the letterbooks comprising series three are indexed.

Series four, 1875–1936, is composed of diaries, appointment

books, school and personal notebooks, scrapbooks, and memorial volumes. Series five through seven, 1880–1937, include his private financial file; donations dockets; and records of real estate, estates, and trusts. Series eight through eleven, 1873–1936, containing papers Mr. and Mrs. McCormick and private secretaries kept in their home office and library, parallel and supplement materials in all of the preceding series. Series twelve, 1903–1935, consists of reports of various committees of the Princeton Board of Trustees. No catalog exists for series four through twelve.

4. McCORMICK, MARY VIRGINIA (1861–1941). PAPERS, 1871–1923. 63 boxes including 64 volumes.

Papers of Mary Virginia McCormick, eldest daughter of Cyrus Hall and Nettie Fowler McCormick who became mentally incompetent at the age of nineteen, consisting of correspondence; early diaries and school notebooks; reports from doctors, nurses, and companions; legal documents; and financial records. These concern relations with members of her family, arrangements for her personal welfare and medical treatment, upkeep of her several homes and estates in the United States and Canada, and plans for travel to her homes and to Europe.

Correspondence describes Virginia's daily activities and state of mind and contains detailed advice concerning her care. Medical letters, reports, and casebooks deal with her mental condition. Legal papers relate to sanity hearings and trusteeships. Financial records include investments; management of her estate; household, personal, and medical bills; and expense accounts. Her papers, ending in the year of her mother's death in 1923, lack any information relating to the last three decades of her life, when she lived chiefly in California as a millionaire recluse with a staff of some thirty persons.

Virginia's mother, her brother Cyrus H. Jr., and her uncle Eldridge M. Fowler, served as original conservators and trustees for her share of the estate inherited from her father; her younger brother and sister, Harold and Anita, were successor trustees; and Judson F. Stone, representing McCormick Estates, managed her financial affairs. In addition to the correspondence of each of these individuals and many who cared for her, the papers include medical case histories and diaries of doctors such as Alice Bennett and Sanger Brown; and letters and reports from Grace T. Walker, head of Virginia's household for forty years.

Organization of the Papers

The Mary Virginia McCormick papers are organized in four series: Correspondence and personal papers, 1871–1922; financial records, 1879–1912; medical reports, 1882–1921; and reports by nurses, 1896–1923. These are arranged by years, and are not cataloged.

5. BLAINE, ANITA McCORMICK (1866–1954). PAPERS, 1828–1958. 1117 boxes including 144 volumes, and 59 volumes.

Papers of Anita McCormick Blaine, philanthropist, consisting of letters, telegrams, and summaries of telephone conversations; reports of committees, boards, and organizations; diaries, speeches, essays, and random notes; financial statements and ledgers; records of investigations; clippings; photographs; blueprints; and a wealth of material relating to personal expenditures and the operation of her household and office. These concern her absorbing interests in education, improvement in social and economic conditions, international understanding, and world peace, and her relations with members of the McCormick family and their friends. Communications from individuals and organizations involved in education, social reform, and foreign affairs added many printed pamphlets and brochures, and typescripts of meetings and speeches to Mrs. Blaine's correspondence files.

Educated by tutors in Europe and New York City and at the Kirkland School in Chicago, in 1889 Anita McCormick married Emmons Blaine, attorney and son of James G. Blaine. Her husband's death in 1892 left her with one son, Emmons, Jr., born in 1890, whom she enrolled in the laboratory school of Cook

County Normal School in 1897. For the next two decades her attention focused chiefly on education and child welfare. Following World War I, Mrs. Blaine's interests expanded to include America's entry into the League of Nations, problems of world peace, and the United Nations. In their treatment of all these interests, her papers are extensive and revealing, demonstrating the depth and breadth of her own involvement both personally and financially.

Her Public Activities and Philanthropies

At about the age of thirty Anita Blaine came under the influence of Francis W. Parker and the movement toward a system of progressive education. Embracing experimental education with characteristic vigor, she conceived of an ideal teacher-training institution under Parker's direction, and the Chicago Institute thus came into being. With Parker as its director; a highly trained and enthusiastic faculty; and a board of trustees composed of Mrs. Blaine, Stanley R. McCormick, Owen F. Addis, Henry Baird Favill, and Cyrus Bentley, the Chicago Institute existed in temporary quarters from 1899 to 1901, when the plans for its buildings and operation proved to be too elaborate even for Mrs. Blaine's generous purse. Her papers contain all records relating to this experimental school, including correspondence, minutes of trustee meetings, memoranda of conferences, financial statements, salary schedules, endowment agreements, and negotiations with the University of Chicago when that institution absorbed the Institute to form its School of Education.

Failing in the original plan to locate her teacher-training project on Chicago's near north side, where children of low-income families could also benefit, Mrs. Blaine nevertheless established the Francis W. Parker elementary school in that area, and assisted its first principal, Flora J. Cooke. Her papers demonstrate the extent to which she gave of her own time to insure its success and contributed to its financial support throughout her life. Between 1905 and 1907 her service as a member of Chicago's Board of Education, with special interest in school management and the selection of textbooks, produced a large file of minutes, reports, recommendations, and correspondence relating to Chicago's public schools.

In pursuit of these early interests in education she corresponded with Wallace W. Atwood, Zonia Baber, Frank M. Bailey, Nicholas Murray Butler, Cornelia B. de Bey, John Dewey, Patrick Geddes, G. Stanley Hall, William Rainey Harper, William T. Harris, Wilbur S. Jackman, and J. G. C. Lee. Although less personally involved, her concern for education expanded to include institutions throughout the country and abroad. For instance, the papers contain correspondence with Robert Maynard Hutchins and Charles H. Judd of the University of Chicago; Clay Judson, trustee for the Francis W. Parker School; Perry Dunlap Smith of the North Shore Country Day School; Carleton W. Washbourne of the Winnetka public schools; and members of the Progressive Education Association. With advice and funds she aided Howard S. Bliss of Protestant College in Beirut; helped Leroy F. Jackson try to revive the defunct Stanley McCormick School with the progressive Carolina New College; encouraged Booker T. Washington at Tuskegee Institute; and responded to the interests of William O. Douglas, Henry R. Luce, and Y. C. James Yen in mass education for China.

Convinced that inherited wealth was a trust to be used in behalf of others—the papers are replete with letters and drafts of ideas expressing this principle—Anita Blaine did not confine her activities to education. Correspondence, reports, speeches, and proposals reveal that she was simultaneously working with individuals involved in child welfare and social reform, particularly in Chicago. For instance, in 1900 she was serving on the board of the city Bureau of Charities and as chairman of the Tenement Committee of the City Homes Association; the following year she publicly supported striking tailors; and in 1906 she was a member of the Juvenile Court and Truancy committees of the Board of Education. Through the years her activities created a large file relating to the Chicago City Council and many of its bureaus and committees.

The papers contain ample evidence of her readiness to express her views to other persons of influence. For example, she sent letters to the city health department arguing for better sanitary inspection; to Mayor Carter H. Harrison protesting exemptions to city ordinances; to Theodore Roosevelt in 1904 giving her opinions on social reform; and to John T. McCutcheon of the Chicago *Tribune,* receiving from him three original political cartoons in addition to his letters of appreciation. In 1936 she appeared on weekly radio in behalf of the Good Neighbor League, as evidenced by correspondence and clippings.

In the field of public concern, correspondence and reports appear in relation to the work of individuals such as Edith and Grace Abbott, Jane Addams, Herman N. Adler, Charles Sumner Bacon, Charles B. Ball, Clifford W. Barnes, Mary M. Bartelme, Gertrude Beeks, Cyrus Bentley, William McCormick Blair, Louise de Koven Bowen, Sophonisba P. Breckinridge, Philip King Brown, Carrie Chapman Catt, Henry P. Chandler, W. E. B. DuBois, Ethel Sturges Dummer, Victor Elting, Arthur Burrage Farwell, Henry Baird Favill, Marshall Field III, Charles Hutchinson, Florence Kelley, Julia C. Lathrop, Cyrus H. and Harriet McCormick, Medill and Ruth Hanna McCormick, Mary E. McDowell, Allen B. Pond, Jacob Riis, Raymond and Margaret Dreier Robins, Anna Howard Shaw, Ellen Gates Starr, Harold F. Swift, Marion Talbot, Graham Taylor, Oswald Garrison Villard, Harriet E. Vittum, and Aubrey Williams; and organizations such as the American Association for Labor Legislation, the American Civic Foundation, the American Social Hygiene Association, the Chicago Bureau of Public Efficiency, the Chicago Council of Social Agencies, the Chicago School of Civics and Philanthropy and its successor the University of Chicago Graduate School of Social Service Administration, the Chicago Urban League, the City Club of Chicago, the Committee of Fifteen to suppress prostitution and organized vice, Hull House, the Institute for Juvenile Research and its publications program called the Behavior Research Fund, the Juvenile Protective Association, the League of Women Voters, the National

Association for the Advancement of Colored People, the National Child Labor Committee and its Illinois chapter, and the Women's Trade Union League of Chicago.

Mrs. Blaine consistently received and responded to appeals from groups such as the American Red Cross seeking aid for relief in European countries, but her greatest interest was in finding means to achieve permanent world peace. The papers include her telegram of October 19, 1920, to President Wilson asking for clarification of the covenant of the League of Nations; and her subsequent open letter, of which copies were printed at her expense and distributed nationally by women's organizations, explaining her support of James M. Cox and the League. Concern for world co-operatoin is reflected in the great number of manuscripts in the 1920's and 1930's relating to organizations such as the American Friends of Turkey, the Chicago Council on Foreign Relations, the Fellowship of Reconciliation, the Institute of Pacific Relations, the League to Enforce Peace for which she was vice-chairman of the Illinois branch, the League of Nations Association, Inc., the League of Nations Non-Partisan Association of which she was at first vice-president, the Women's International League for Peace and Freedom, and the World Foundation.

Extensive materials describe the World Citizens Association, organized in 1938 in her home, to research and publicize the need for world co-operation. She served the association as vice-chairman, contributed funds, and co-authored *The World at the Crossroads*. With the approach of World War II, the papers pertain also to her work on the executive committee of the International Rescue Committee to aid refugees from Fascist countries, and her support of the Committee to Defend America by Aiding the Allies. In May, 1941, her published letter urging United States entry into the war brought a flood of responses from citizens, to many of which she replied. (These are filed under the name of Mrs. Emmons Blaine.) Her work on the board of the American Association for the United Nations is documented, and her telegram to the San Francisco organizing conference, counseling compromise on the veto, is included. In 1947 she began meeting and corresponding with Evanston and Chicago leaders of World Republic, intending to make annual contributions "until the objective is reached and world government is a fact." The following June she helped plan and finance the Pocono Pines (Pennsylvania) Conference to discuss extra-governmental ways to resolve differences between peoples. Out of this came her million-dollar gift to the Foundation for World Government, for which her papers contain the Foundation's correspondence, minutes, speeches, memoranda, agreements, bank statements, records of grants, and audits.

During the three decades of her search for international understanding, through what she always hoped would be more than paper organizations, Mrs. Blaine corresponded with individuals such as Harland H. Allen, Courtenay Barber, Jr., Stringfellow Barr, Frank G. Baudreau, Charles C. Bauer, Stephen Benedict, Philip Bennett, Henri Bonnet, Edward C. Carter, Edwin H. Cassels, John H. Clarke, Edwin M. Clough, Everett Colby, Ruth Cranston, William E. Dodd, Paul H. and Emily Taft Douglas, Paul Draper, Clark M. Eichelberger, Edwin R. Embree, Fyke Farmer, Frederick V. Field, Irving Fisher, Charles W. Gilkey, Roger S. Greene, Stuart Hayden, Manley O. Hudson, Asa K. Jennings, Florence Jennison, Paul U. Kellogg, Walter H. C. Laves, Salvador de Madariaga, Edgar Ansel Mower, Eleanor Roosevelt, William H. Short, Arthur Swetser, Henry Usborne, William Allen White, George W. Wickersham, Ray Lyman Wilbur, Harris Wofford, Mary E. Woolley, and Quincy Wright. Final attempts to influence the course of thought and action is evidenced by her 1949 pledge to help finance the New York *Daily Compass,* and correspondence with its publisher, T. O. Thackery; and, by her will, the creation of a twenty-million-dollar trust for her New World Foundation.

Scattered letters indicate early vacillation between her husband's Republican party and traditional McCormick family affiliation with the Democratic party, although her convictions usually bound her to the latter. She received letters from Theodore Roosevelt while he was governor of New York, and corresponded with Woodrow Wilson, Herbert Hoover, Franklin D. Roosevelt, and Harry S. Truman. She had Roosevelt's Chautauqua speech on foreign relations (1936) printed for distribution, and addressed the nation by radio in his behalf in 1940. Correspondence relating to politics and other matters was carried on with men such as John Peter Altgeld, Joseph E. Davies, Arthur Goldberg, Frank O. Lowden, John T. McManus, Charles E. Merriam, James G. Patton, and Adlai E. Stevenson II. Correspondence with C. B. Baldwin and Sidney Hillman, and her service with the women's division of the Illinois Political Action Committee, led her to become one of the moving forces in creation of the Progressive party. For the Henry A. Wallace presidential campaign of 1948 a file contains correspondence with Wallace and others, memoranda of meetings in her home, speeches, and records of her large contributions.

In addition to causes that claimed most of her attention, the papers contain a variety of materials relating to many other philanthropies and interests. For instance, she corresponded with James G. K. McClure, Sr., John Timothy Stone, and Andrew C. Zenos of the McCormick Theological Seminary in Chicago; Charles Oliver Gray of Tusculum College; Chauncey B. McCormick concerning the Art Institute of Chicago and Polish relief; Fletcher S. Brockman, Sherwood Eddy, and John R. Mott regarding the Young Men's Christian Association, foreign students, and Eddy's Southern co-operative projects and lectures for the United Service Organizations (USO); Harriet Taylor of the Young Women's Christian Association; Dwight L. Moody and Emma Dryer relating to their Bible work; Henry Winters Luce concerning Peking University in China; William Plumer Jacobs of the Thornwell Orphanage in South Carolina; James G. K. McClure, Jr. of the Farmer's Federation of North Carolina; and Henry Van Dyke of Princeton. She received letters and reports from psychiatrists Adolf Meyer and William Alanson White, and cooperated with her brothers in contributing to psychiatric research at Johns Hopkins University. A large gift to the Chinese people in 1943 was followed by notes from Madame Chiang Kai-shek, to whom she presented the fund. Although there is evidence that institutional religion was less important to her than to her mother, the papers show much concern for her own Fourth Presbyterian Church, the ministerial fund, and mission work of the Presbyterian Church in the United States.

Her Family, Friends, and Financial Affairs

Letters, clippings, photographs, ledgers, and memoranda concerning her family and personal business comprise a large part of the Anita Blaine papers. These show her to have been in close contact with her mother and brothers, as might be expected in a closely knit family where each person felt similar responsibilities and shared in the income from a large and growing business. Because the activities, finances, and trusteeships of Nettie McCormick and her children Cyrus, Jr., Anita, and Harold were so interlocking, they held many conferences, for most of which minutes are filed, and frequently wrote each other of matters common to all. As a trustee for the care and estates of her incompetent sister and brother, Virginia and Stanley, voluminous correspondence was carried on by Anita with their many companions, doctors, and lawyers, particularly on behalf of Virginia. The papers also contain evidence of Anita's continuance of the Family Gift Syndicate, the McCormick Historical Association, and the Nettie Fowler McCormick Biographical Association long after the deaths of her brothers.

The papers of Emmons Blaine are on file, although these, and correspondence with Anita, are limited in amount due to his early death. Letters and business records of Mrs. Blaine's son, who was educated at Harvard University and chose agriculture in Wisconsin as a career, are much more extensive. The death of Emmons, Jr., at the age of twenty-eight left her to carry on the operation of his Milford Meadows Stock Farm through agents until 1947, at which time she gave it and a trust fund to the University of Wisconsin. In addition, the papers include years of correspondence with her only grandchild, Anne

(Nancy) Blaine, now the wife of Gilbert A. Harrison, editor of the *New Republic*. Many records appear concerning conferences among Mrs. Harrison, lawyers, and secretaries in the years just preceding and following the death of Mrs. Blaine.

In addition to a large number of friends, Mrs. Blaine corresponded with many members of the Adams, Blaine, and McCormick families, including her husband's parents; his sisters, Harriet Blaine Beale and Margaret Blaine Damrosh; and the widow of Emmons, Jr., Eleanor Blaine Lawrence. Among the most personal and confidential letters are those she wrote to her childhood governess, Harriot M. Hammond, prior to 1904. Letters from her mother's secretary, Truman B. Gorton, and biographer, Virginia Roderick, are numerous; so also are letters and reports from the curator of the McCormick Historical Association, Herbert A. Kellar. In behalf of her many projects she received letters and landscape designs from Warren H. Manning. Included in her correspondence are also letters from Britishers interested in psychic phenomena—Helen V. Alvey, Arthur Conan Doyle, and Oliver Lodge—a subject that increasingly intrigued her in her later years.

Files of Cyrus Bentley and his son, Richard, and those of McCormick Estates and the International Harvester Company provide the most complete record of Mrs. Blaine's financial situation. As her friend and personal attorney, Cyrus Bentley helped manage her business affairs and took an active part in many of the same organizations as she. Richard Bentley became her adviser after his father's death in 1930, and with Mrs. Harrison was executor for her estate. Additional financial and legal information appears in the files of Cyrus Bentley's partner, Edwin H. Cassels, and his secretary, Emil Christiansen. The papers also contain correspondence, memoranda, and reports from her bank, the Merchants Loan & Trust Company; from Charles F. Farrell, a business agent; from George W. Perkins of the International Harvester Company; and from George H. Sullivan and John Hays Hammond, advisers on investments and other legal matters.

Her Household and Office

Mrs. Blaine spent and gave away so much money, and was involved in so many activities, that her Chicago mansion, where she lived alone much of the time, took on the aspects of an institution as well as a home; and in 1928 she set up an office in the Farwell Building. In these two places causes were initiated, plans were made, and conferences were held, for all of which records were always kept. As early as 1900 she shocked the business world by instituting an eight-hour day for her staff, and through the following half-century she annually employed as many as five to nine servants and three to five secretaries.

Seldom do an individual's papers exhibit, in quantity and detail, so much information concerning daily living and office procedure as do those of Anita Blaine. Written messages constantly flowed between her and her servants and secretaries. The papers contain household accounts, orders, and shopping lists; assignment of duties and directions for carrying them out; reports on work accomplished and problems encountered; recommendations from both employer and staff; and telephone messages coming into the home. Concerning her office the papers include methods outlined for its management, diaries and reports of secretaries, questions and recommendations, summaries of telephone conversations, gift information with annotations as to Mrs. Blaine's intent, and press releases.

Organization of the Papers

The Anita McCormick Blaine papers are organized in five series, with the contents of folders generally arranged as Mrs. Blaine's secretaries maintained them. Thus, in addition to the unbound manuscripts, the file boxes of all five series contain a large number of volumes varying greatly in size and content relating to her personal life and the operation of her household and office. Forty-three of the numbered volumes not filed in boxes consist chiefly of financial ledgers; but they include also two volumes of letters and photographs of the Chicago Institute, one volume concerning World Republic, and an album of photographs of the 1912 Child Welfare Exhibit.

Series one, 1828–1957, consists of letters, memoranda, telegrams, reports, minutes, speeches, pamphlets, and brochures received by Mrs. Blaine. It is organized by individual or subject and is accompanied by an alphabetical index of folder titles. Series two, 1871–1958, concerns Mrs. Blaine's own letters and writings, is organized chronologically, and has no index. The first part contains her own letters, memoranda, telephone conversations, notes on meetings, speeches, essays, and poems. The remainder consists of address books, checkbook stubs, representative samples of memoranda books in which she jotted ideas, lists, and expenses; photographs; publications by her; and press clippings documenting her public and private life.

Series three, 1896–1957, concerns the operation of her household; and series four, 1889–1952, the operation and work of her office. Both series are in order by years, but have no index.

Series five, 1850–1958, parallels series two, having been held apart from her other papers until given to the Society by her granddaughter in 1971. Filed in this series are Mrs. Blaine's own diaries, which changed in character after about 1910 to become jotted philosophical ideas and unfinished thoughts on religion; some of her most private correspondence; and information relating to her own estate and those of her husband and son. In addition, the papers of Emmons Blaine and Emmons Blaine, Jr., are included in this series.

6. McCormick, Harold F. (1872–1941). Papers, 1892–1947. 90 boxes including 12 volumes, and 1 volume.

Papers of Harold F. McCormick, Chicago industrialist, consisting of correspondence, notes, business records, appointment books, speeches, clippings, and printed items. These concern financial interests, civic groups, personal and family life, and his publicized peace plan during World War I. One-third of the papers predate 1910; the smallest number cover the two decades of his greatest activity in Chicago business and civic affairs; and one-half postdates 1930. A minor portion consists of papers of his daughter, Muriel, including her interest in postwar relief work, the theater, and Chicago grand opera.

His Business Interests

Following graduation from Princeton University in 1895, Mc-Cormick joined the McCormick Harvesting Machine Company as sales manager at Council Bluffs, Iowa, for which one letter-book and some unbound correspondence are filed. Returning to Chicago in 1898, he became vice-president of the Company, a position he retained when the International Harvester Company was formed in 1902; succeeded Cyrus, H., Jr., as president of International Harvester in 1918; served as chairman of the executive committee between 1922 and 1932; and succeeded his brother as chairman of the board in 1935. Correspondence, business records, and appointment books relating to the parent company, and to McCormick Estates, appear in his early papers, but any material concerning the International Harvester Company is scattered and peripheral. Filed with the volumes are manuscripts for books by Cyrus Bentley and Robert H. Parkinson on the history of the reaper.

With the exception of agreements, correspondence, reports and accounts of the Belle City Malleable Iron Company at Racine, Wisconsin, acquired in 1899, all business records are sparse; although correspondence with his financial agents includes references to his many Chicago properties, and to stock invested in enterprises such as the Chicago Hardware Company, the East Chicago Company, the Calumet Canal and Dock Company, various railroads, and western mines. Among his business and legal correspondents were G. H. Carver, John A. Chapman, Paul D. Cravath, John C. Fetzer, Eldridge M. Fowler, J. J. Glessner, John Hays Hammond, E. H. Hanfstaengl, Turlington W. Harvey, John R. Hoagland, W. S. Krebs, Alexander Legge, Cyrus H. McCormick, Jr., Addis E. McKinstry, Hiram B. Prentice, George A. Ranney, Judson F. Stone, and the First National Bank of Chicago, of which he was a director.

His Public Service and Philanthropies

McCormick's correspondence demonstrates his interest in a wide variety of civic activities and philanthropies, with substantial material appearing for the Merchants Club and Commercial Club, particularly their projects to develop the Chicago Plan for urban improvement and to locate the Naval Training Station; the Chicago Plan Commission; the John Rockefeller McCormick Institute for Infectious Diseases, established by McCormick and his wife in 1902 as a memorial to their son; the University of Chicago and its committees, of which he was a trustee for four decades; and Olivet Institute, of which he was chairman of the board. Contributions to many charities are shown, and scattered letters concern reform movements in Chicago, Democratic party finances and candidates, the McCormick Theological Seminary, Princeton University, Washington and Lee University, and the Young Men's Christian Association. Correspondents include Jane Addams, Norman B. Barr, Gertrude Beeks, Frank Billings, Louise de Koven Bowen, Charles R. Crane, William Rainey Harper, Ludwig Hekloen, Robert Maynard Hutchins, Herrick Johnson, Harry Pratt Judson, Rollin A. Keyes, Henry Winters Luce, James G. K. McClure, Sr., Chauncey B. McCormick, Medill and Ruth Hanna McCormick, Mary E. McDowell, Warren H. Manning, Charles E. Merriam, John R. Mott, Richard C. Morse, Potter Palmer, John Timothy Stone, and Graham Romeyn Taylor.

The papers contain McCormick's letters, notes, printed brochure, and reminiscences describing his peace plan, *Via Pacis,* developed in Switzerland in 1915, including correspondence with Jules Cambon, Edouard Dujardin, Edward M. House, and Elihu Root. Included also are his personal account of German peace terms he carried to Woodrow Wilson in 1918; correspondence with Charles G. Dawes, for whom he served as procurement officer; and letters concerning the League to Enforce Peace and the League of Nations Association.

His Family and Personal Interests

Correspondence appears frequently with members of the Mc-Cormick family, particularly with his mother, his brother Cyrus, Jr., and his sister Anita, dealing with their interlocking financial interests, family conferences, and philanthropies. The papers contain many clippings concerning, but lack correspondence with, each of his three wives—Edith Rockefeller, whom he married in 1895; Ganna Walska, Polish diva whom he married in 1922; and Adah Wilson, his nurse whom he married in 1938. Letters of his children—Fowler, Mathilde, and Muriel—are also rare, with the exception of the latter's own papers for 1920 to 1925.

Both family and business connections led him to correspond with John D. Rockefeller, and John D., Jr.; and he regularly received letters and reports from Walter and Rush Searson who operated "Walnut Grove," the ancestral home in Virginia acquired by Harold.* The files contain many letters exchanged with doctors and clinics, especially in relation to arthritis or psychiatric treatment.

McCormick's papers confirm his reputation as a patron of music, to which he gave organizational time and financial support, keeping files relating to the Civic Music Association of Chicago, the Chicago Orchestral Association, the Chicago Symphony Orchestra Association, the Chicago Opera Association, and the Chicago Civic Opera Company; corresponding with performing artists such as Cleofonte Campanini and Mary Garden; and writing a series of articles for the Chicago *Daily News* called "The Story of Grand Opera in Chicago" (1935). Enthusiasm for aviation, particularly the development of the Vertaplane, led him to communicate with E. Hicks Herrick, Gerardus P. Herrick, and others as early as 1901 and to encourage aircraft experi-

---

*In 1954 the heirs of Harold F. McCormick presented the "Walnut Grove" land and buildings to the Virginia Polytechnic Institute as the site for its Shenandoah Valley Research Station. The home provides offices; and the restored mill and forge, where the reaper was invented, are open to the public.

ments; and records of European trips early in the century attest to his devotion to the development of the automobile. As a national amateur racquets champion, his interest in this and other sports is mirrored in the papers.

Organization of the Papers

The Harold F. McCormick papers are organized in two series. The first, 1892–1947, contains McCormick's own papers, organized chronologically and indexed as to chronology, names of individuals, and subjects. The second series, 1920–1925, is composed of Muriel's papers, arranged by year and not indexed.

7. McCORMICK, STANLEY R. (1874–1947). PAPERS, 1881–1945. 15 boxes including 6 volumes

Papers of Stanley R. McCormick, youngest son of Cyrus Hall and Nettie Fowler McCormick, who became mentally incompetent at the age of thirty-two, consisting of correspondence, notes, minutes, financial accounts, medical reports and charts, legal documents, and transcripts of court hearings. These concern his early business interests, arrangements for his care, controversies between the McCormicks and his wife Katherine, whom he married in 1904, and reports of medical consultants.

Following his graduation from Princeton University in 1895, poor health and a desire to study art took him to Europe, but he soon returned to join the McCormick Harvesting Machine Company, first as a salesman and then as comptroller. The papers contain business letters of 1899 and 1900, chiefly in the latter year when he represented the Company at the Paris exposition and corresponded with his Chicago office, his brothers Cyrus, Jr. and Harold, their competitor James Deering, and the Company manager in Hamburg, Germany, W. V. Couchman. A few letters and accounts appear relating to his Cimarron Ranch on the historic Maxwell Land Grant in New Mexico, acquired in 1898 with John W. Garrett but later developed by McCormick.

The bulk of the papers deal with the many problems concerning McCormick's care after his breakdown in 1906, and his progressive incapacitation due to a mental disease diagnosed as catatonia. In addition to letters of his wife, members of the McCormick family, and a few friends, correspondence of doctors and psychiatrists such as Frank Billings, Henry Baird Favill, C. G. Jung, Adolf Meyer, and George Tuttle is included, as is a special medical evaluation by August Hoch and Emil Kraepelin. Medical correspondence, reports by nurses and staff, minutes of the board of guardians, financial accounts, and arrangements for his care at the spacious California home provided him are all filed. Four volumes contain court proceedings of 1929–1930 regarding the question of guardianship and his multimillion-dollar estate.

Organization of the Papers

The Stanley R. McCormick papers are organized in five series. Series one, 1881–1931, consists of business and family correspondence; series two, 1923–1929, correspondence and reports of those responsible for his care; series three, 1930–1945, minutes of the board of guardians and opinions of medical consultants; series four, 1928–1930, legal papers and court hearings; and series five, 1906–1933, medical reports. The first series is arranged by years, with letters filed alphabetically by author within each year; and the remaining series are arranged by months. No series is cataloged.

McCORMICK
COMPANY PAPERS

8. McCormick Harvesting Machine Company. Papers, 1618–1909. 655 boxes, and 1110 volumes and 1 package.

Papers of the McCormick Harvesting Machine Company, consisting of correspondence, reports, financial accounts, legal and patent records, and advertising. These cover the half-century of its existence, from the time when Cyrus Hall McCormick produced his first reapers in Chicago until the Company consolidated with four other firms to form the International Harvester Company in 1902.*

Correspondence and Reports

Letters to agents, shippers, suppliers, lawyers, and other manufacturers appear in letterbooks, of which 455 contain chiefly domestic correspondence, 1856–1902, and seventeen deal entirely with the foreign trade, 1879–1902. These tissue copies of *outgoing* communications, which improve in readability and detail after the Company adopted the typewriter in 1882, clearly demonstrate the growth of the McCormick companies, as do the *incoming* communications, 1848–1909, contained in 642 archival boxes and one volume. This correspondence is mainly confined to the manufacture and distribution of farm machinery, reflect-

*For titles by which the Company was known prior to 1879, see page 2.

ing agricultural development and changes in rural life but rarely discussing political or other social problems.

Company letters to representatives in the field deal with production goals, machines manufactured and shipped, arrangements for providing parts and twine, field trials and performance of implements, freight routes and costs, prices and contracts, expected sales, collection policies, problems with competitors and unreliable agents, expectations from harvests, extension of the implement trade, and agent expenses. Relatively few letters are signed by Cyrus H. McCormick, although many appearing in the Company name in early years may well have been written at his direction. Officers wrote him when he was absent from Chicago, and their letters to agents sometimes quoted him. Of his partners, the influence of his brother, William S., is evident, since William was in charge of the office until his death in 1865; and letters of Cyrus H. McCormick, Jr., especially concerning the foreign market, appear after he joined the Company in 1879. Through the years, officers and secretaries, some of whom started as agents in the field, were responsible for most of the Company's general correspondence; they include E. K. Butler, D. W. Cobb, William J. Hanna, William Howard, W. S. Krebs, Alexander Legge, Harold F. McCormick, Stanley R. McCormick, F. H. Mathews, William Mathews, William C. Mundt, Herbert F. Perkins, W. R. Selleck, Charles R. Spring, Jr., and James P. Whedon.

Agent letters and reports to the Company deal with trade extension, competitive practices in local areas, the price and performance of machines, sales contracts, collection of notes, crop yields, insect and disease or weather damage to crops, complaints of farmers, and Grange activities in the 1870's. Because so many distributors corresponded with the office over such a long period, any selected list of agents risks being misleading. However, a few may be noted as illustrative of the scope of the correspondence: H. C. Addis and H. R. Gould in Nebraska; N. E. Barnes in California and the Arizona Territory; E. C. Beardsley, first in Illinois and then in Minnesota; S. L. Beardsley in Michigan; Consolidated Implement Company in Utah; H. N. Johnston in New York; and John B. McCormick and Patrick Mohan, first in Kentucky and then in Missouri. Traveling collecting agents such as Angus Stewart sent in reports on the financial status of farmers and conditions affecting their ability to meet payments. To expand its foreign markets, the Company sent Edward A. Ackerman to investigate possibilities in New Zealand, Australia, and southern Africa; and maintained agents such as Agar, Cross & Co. in Scotland, W. V. Couchman in Germany, Lankester & Co. in England, McLean Bros. & Rigg in Australia, George A. Freudenreich in Russia, and Wesbrook & Fairchild in Canada.

The papers contain many communications with railroads relating to routes and rates, and arrangements with shipping brokers such as Norton & Son in New York and Henry W. Peabody & Co. in Boston. Procurement of supplies and equipment accounts for correspondence with companies providing products such as lumber, belting, iron, bolts, and nuts. Orders for knives and sickles went out to other manufacturers, and the McCormick Company made arrangements with cordage producers in obtaining and selling twine. The constant struggle with patent infringements produced correspondence with inventors and other implement companies such as Sylvanus D. Lockes and D. M. Osborne & Company; and with lawyers and patent experts such as William D. Baldwin, Joseph G. and Robert H. Parkinson, and R. B. Swift. In addition, many applications for employment appear with the correspondence, as do land titles, deeds, and mortgages. Material for 1902 to 1904 includes reports and contracts of parent companies after they formed and became divisions of the International Harvester Company.

Financial Accounts

Financial records, 1848–1904, of the McCormick Harvesting Machine Company, in varying detail and often in broken sequence, include virtually every phase of its operation. An indication of the coverage is provided in the following lists, with the 410 volumes grouped as to subject matter and date.

General accounts deal with receipts and expenditures of all kinds—sales, repairs, office supplies, purchases, wages, expense accounts, and equipment. Agency records include agents, areas, commissions, salaries, expenses, and reports on payments for machines; also reapers, mowers, rakes, and parts delivered and sold. Customer accounts show individual purchasers and agents in various states. Factory records include production, sales, and shipments expressed in physical volume, unit costs, consignee, customers, supplies required, and inventories. By departments (e.g., reaper, sickle, paint, foundry, brass) payroll records give employee names, work periods, rates, days worked or piece work, and total pay. Twine accounts list types and volume of twine sold, agents and customers to whom shipped, terms of transactions, value, and purchases from or sales to other companies. Real estate and rentals include locations, transactions, and taxes for the Company; and detailed information on purchases in behalf of C. H. McCormick and his brothers in the 1860's.

In the following lists, numbers on the right represent total volumes:

GENERAL ACCOUNTS

Cash receipts and expenditures	1848–1873	12
Journal of transactions	1848–1873	17
Ledger of all accounts	1848–1873	14
Partners' interests and accounts	1860–1879	1
Expense accounts	1862–1867	1
Cash daily balance	1866–1874	1
Reaper expenses, manufacture and sales	1868–1870	1
Trial balances, 1866; collections	1871–1873	1
Barter accounts, debits and credits	1873–1886	4
Daybook of purchases	1900–1901	1
Boarding house operation—workmen	1900–1901	1
Cash receipts and disbursements	1900–1901	5
Cash daily balance	1900–1901	1
Voucher register, manufacture, agents	1900–1901	1

Voucher register, all accounts	1900–1902	1
Check register	1900–1902	4
Ledger: general, maintenance, manufacturing	1901–1904	2

AGENCY RECORDS

Deliveries to agents	1851–1873	23
Agencies by name and location	1857–1868	4
Agency transportation costs	1859–1870	1
Collection register	1863–1902	34
Machines and parts ordered	1864–1876	8
Machines received. Inventories	1870–1902	11
Annual settlements by agents	1876–1903	25
Reports on sub-agents	1899–1902	3
Repairs and parts ledger	1901–1902	1
Agency salaries and expenses	1901–1902	1
Insurance coverage on stock	1901–1902	1

CUSTOMER ACCOUNTS

Notes, renewals, collections	1848–1903	4
Bills receivable	1849–1884	42

FACTORY PRODUCTION, SALES, SHIPMENTS

Sales—volume and consignee	1849–1872	1
Orders—volume and consignee (agents)	1851–1874	16
Sales—volume, price, model	1854–1872	13
Machine parts shipped	1857–1864	4
Stock inventory—machines	1860–1879	1
Annual porduction; machines returned	1862–1875	4
Railroad freight rates (printed)	1863–1873	2
Supplies required	1872, 1874	2
Stock inventory—machines, supplies	1899	1
Lumber purchased	1900–1901	1
Machine and rake shipments	1900–1902	4
Machine shipments from works	1900–1903	3

PAYROLL RECORDS

Departments, employees, wages, time	1858–1901	106
Office—employees, rates of pay	1899–1902	3
Foundry—employees, rates of pay	1900–1901	2
Foremen and assistants, rates of pay	1900–1902	2

TWINE ACCOUNTS		
Twine volume, value, customer	1888–1899	1
Twine costs, sales, volume	1891–1901	1
Twine to agents and customers	1899–1900	1
Shipments, by carrier and consignee	1900–1902	1
Twine inventory, factory and field	1902	1
REAL ESTATE AND RENTALS		
Property taxes, Illinois	1858–1873	1
McCormick lands in four states	1862–1865	1
McCormick lands; owner, loans, taxes	1862–1863	1
Rents collected	1863–1872	5
Real estate journals and ledgers	1873–1904	5

Legal and Patent Records

Early and continuing controversies with other inventors and implement manufacturers is evidenced by the large number of printed volumes and drawings accumulated by the Company in dealing with lawsuits. These are composed of briefs, records, arguments, exhibits, and specifications used in proceedings before civil courts and the U. S. Patent Office. Included also are descriptions of McCormick family patents; volumes showing the history of agricultural machinery patents, some dating back to seventeenth-century Britain; and a manuscript book of the McCormicks' own assignor-assignee patent records between 1860 and 1880.

Advertising, Catalogs, and Expositions

One bound volume of dealers' catalogs for McCormick farm equipment, 1880–1900, appears with the papers, as do many advertising leaflets, brochures, and promotional materials. Miscellaneous clippings, 1867–1885, include the strike of 1885. The importance the Company attached to the need to exhibit its products and compete at international expositions accounts for many volumes of descriptive guides, catalogs, directories, judges' decisions and commissioners' reports published in connection with such events. One manuscript volume lists all exhibits by the McCormick Harvesting Machine Company at the Paris International Exposition of 1900.

Organization of the Papers

The McCormick Harvesting Machine Company Papers are organized in six series. The letterbooks of series one, 1856–1902, are indexed; and the incoming correspondence, reports, and contracts of series two, 1848–1909, are accompanied by a partial card catalog. An inventory is filed describing each of the financial volumes comprising series three, 1848–1904. Series four through six, 1618–1900, are composed of patent records, advertising, and exposition materials—chiefly printed volumes and brochures.

9. INTERNATIONAL HARVESTER COMPANY. PAPERS, 1834–1967. 34 boxes, and 691 volumes.

Papers of the International Harvester Company, formed in August, 1902, by a consolidation of the McCormick Harvesting Machine Company, the Deering Harvester Company, and the Plano Manufacturing Company, all in the Chicago area; the Milwaukee Harvester Company in Wisconsin; and the Warder, Bushnell, & Glessner Company (Champion) at Springfield, Ohio. International Harvester thus came into control of the country's harvesting equipment, with about 90 per cent of its grain-binder production and 80 per cent of its mowers, the two chief harvesting machines.

The papers consist of business reports, financial accounts, legal and patent records, advertising, and catalogs—some relating to International Harvester itself, and some concerning its parent companies and their rivals prior to consolidation.* Included also are a few miscellaneous records of two of several other companies soon acquired by International Harvester; namely, D. M. Osborne & Company, Auburn, New York, and the Keystone

---

*One exception is the McCormick Harvesting Machine Company, for which all records prior to consolidation are contained in that company's papers.

Company, Rock Falls, Illinois. No correspondence appears in the papers; and with the exception of the 621 manuscript volumes of financial accounts, the material is virtually all in printed form.

Business Records

Business records contain various reports concerning the International Harvester Company consisting of charter and by-laws, 1902, 1904, 1918; minutes, 1902; incorporation documents, 1907; annual reports for 1907 through 1966; a history of the Company, 1902–1913, by the U. S. Department of Commerce and Labor, and its anti-trust committee reports for 1913; a confidential statement of the Company for the 1920 season; sales and collection organization charts, 1926–1929; an accountants' report, 1927; arbitration decisions on labor relations, 1943–1955; telegraphic code, 1947; quarterly reports, 1965–1967; and for varying years, reports of the president, meetings of shareholders, and employee pension benefits. Included also are miscellaneous papers of D. M. Osborne & Company, 1883–1885, and its sale agreement, 1902; and miscellaneous papers of the Deering Harvester Company, 1893, and a Deering appraisal, 1903.

Financial Accounts

Financial records, 1881–1949, of the International Harvester Company are concerned chiefly with those of the parent companies before they consolidated in 1902, and as they later operated as divisions of International Harvester. The 621 volumes are grouped by subject matter and date.

Agency records vary with company and division; but in general they include names and locations, salaries, and domestic and foreign sales. The Company's annual settlement records contain comprehensive reports on volume, expenses, sales, collections, and balances, chiefly by general agents and districts. *Factory production and sales* volumes describe shop orders, materials, job completions, salaries, and operating expenses. *Payroll records* include time, pay, and expenses for workers in various divisions and departments, with more than half of the total volumes relating to the McCormick Division of International Harvester. In the following lists, numbers on the right represent total volumes.

AGENCY RECORDS

Deering Harvester Company
    Roadmen—name, salary, contracts, sales   1892–1902   14
Milwaukee Harvester Company
    Agents—locations, contracts, salary   1898–1901   1
Champion Division, IHC
    Agencies and sales—domestic, foreign   1903   1
International Harvester Company
    Annual settlement with agents   1904–1913   106

FACTORY PRODUCTION AND SALES

McCormick Division, IHC
    Special order ledger (red order)   1902–1904   3
    Shop order ledger   1905–1949   32
    Factory ledger; some office accounts   1906–1944   8
Deering Division, IHC
    Factory and shop order ledger   1932–1947   5

PAYROLL RECORDS

Deering Harvester Company
    Office records of company payrolls   1883–1901   7
    Foundries—time book and payrolls   1889–1902   20
    Twine time book and payrolls   1895–1902   21
    Employee records   1896 (?), 1935–1938   2
    Office time books   1896–1901   6
    Factory time and payrolls   1898–1902   24
Plano Manufacturing Company
    Time and payrolls   1881–1902   21
    Time book   1891–1894   1
    Twine mill time and payrolls   1899–1900   2
Plano Division, IHC
    Time and payroll records   1903–1908   9
    Payrolls, construction pay, profits   1904–1922
        (on microfilm)   7 reels

McCormick Division, IHC

Payrolls—clerks, foremen, assistants	1899–1919	5
Private payrolls	1902–1939	27
IHC payrolls, McCormick Works	1902–1940	298
Cash book, employee expenses	1903–1904	1
Special private payrolls (None for 1927–1929)	1920–1935	2
Payrolls—factory foremen, assistants	1923–1931	1
Milwaukee Harvester Company Time and payroll books	1900–1902	3
Keystone Company Payroll books	1902–1906	2

Legal and Patent Records

Patent suits account for several court briefs, opinions, and exhibits, 1907–1911, n.d., but by far the greatest number of legal volumes in the International Harvester Company papers are concerned with the records of hearings and proceedings, 1912–1922, concerning the federal government's anti-trust suit against the Company. These include also a history of the litigation, and a catalog of volumes relating to the International Harvester Company vs. the United States in anti-trust suits.

Advertising, Catalogs, and Expositions

The papers contain a large number of catalogs, brochures, and leaflets describing the expanding line of International Harvester Company products, from all kinds of agricultural machinery to tractors and motor trucks. These include miscellaneous unbound catalogs, 1902–1961, for International Harvester; nine bound volumes of general catalogs, 1920–1961; seven bound volumes of distributors' catalogs—five containing the undated earliest publications, one for 1911, and one for 1945; three export general catalogs, Nos. 125, 131, 140; eight volumes of catalogs and price lists for International Motor Trucks, 1914–1940; eight volumes of catalogs, price lists, and repair parts for Deering equipment, 1897–1920; and miscellaneous catalogs for repair parts.

Notes and descriptions concerning exhibits in expositions, 1906–1936, are included, as are all 1920 issues of *The Main Wheel* published by the Deering twine mill, clippings for 1901 to 1928, two volumes of lecture notes on International Harvester equipment, and one volume of the Company's agricultural bulletins. In addition, the papers contain a large collection of advertising circulars, leaflets, and brochures produced by many agricultural implement manufacturers dating back to Obed Hussey's reapers of 1834, all filed by name of company or inventor.

Organization of the Papers

The International Harvester Company papers are organized in four series. Series one is composed of business records, 1883–1885, 1893, 1902–1967; series two, 1881–1949, contains financial ledgers and accounts; series three, 1907–1922, includes legal and patent records; and series four, 1834–1961, is composed of advertising, catalogs, and notes on exhibits at expositions.

10. REAPER CENTENNIAL CELEBRATION. PAPERS, *ca.* 1926–1933. 33 boxes, and 30 volumes.

Papers of the International Harvester Company's 1931 centennial celebration of McCormick's invention of the reaper, consisting of correspondence, committee reports, clippings, and photographs. Correspondence is chiefly that of members of the McCormick family, officials of International Harvester, Herbert A. Kellar of the McCormick Historical Association, planning committees, and representatives responsible for managing and reporting on the event in the United States and abroad. Hundreds of clippings, mounted and unmounted, deal with advance publicity, scholarship awards, and coverage of celebration activities in practically every state and many foreign countries. Five volumes of photographs picture the development of McCormick harvesting machines and events commemorating the centennial, including special observances at Washington and Lee University and Virginia Polytechnic Institute.

11. AMERICAN HARVESTER COMPANY. PAPERS, 1889–1890, 1899. 3 boxes including 2 volumes.

Papers of a proposed nineteenth-century merger of the principal manufacturers of harvesters and mowers in the United States under the title of American Harvester Company, consisting of correspondence, inventories, contracts, minutes, resolutions of meetings, and clippings. Organized in November of 1890, the consolidation never was consummated and plans were abandoned early in January of 1891.

The papers contain communications and agreements with some eighteen companies, most of the correspondence being that of officers designated to head the proposed combine: Cyrus H. McCormick, Jr., president; William Deering, chairman of the board; E. K. Butler, general manager; and Arthur L. Conger, assistant general manager. One letter, February 10, 1899, concerns purchase of options Conger obtained in 1890 from participating companies, and his suggestions for a new attempt at consolidation.

McCORMICK
HISTORICAL
RECORDS

12. McCORMICK BIOGRAPHICAL ASSOCIATION. PAPERS, 1896–1912.
5 boxes including 2 volumes.

Correspondence and records of the McCormick Biographical Association, formed after the death of Cyrus Hall McCormick by his widow and children to insure and perpetuate his role in industrial and agricultural history. Secretaries collected and cataloged publications and manuscripts; replied to numerous genealogical inquiries; provided information to authors such as McCormick's earliest biographer, Herbert N. Casson; helped arrange for a monograph on McCormick by Reuben Gold Thwaites; gathered evidence to present to the New York University Hall of Fame; and supervised a McCormick display at the Jamestown Exposition of 1907. In 1912, this association was succeeded by the McCormick Historical Association.

13. McCORMICK HISTORICAL ASSOCIATION. PAPERS, 1892–1963.
42 boxes.

Administrative correspondence and records of the McCormick Historical Association, formed in 1912 and financed by the children of Cyrus Hall McCormick to collect and preserve papers relating to their father, his companies, and his contemporaries. The papers reflect chiefly the work of Herbert A. Kellar, who became curator for the association in 1915, and Lucile O'Connor Kellar, later his research associate. They and their assistants replied to numerous historical and genealogical inquiries; sought out, secured, and cataloged many publications and collateral collections; compiled information concerning the reaper, agriculture, and Virginia; supervised McCormick-related projects such as the "Walnut Grove" restoration in Virginia, 1937–1938; provided information to authors such as McCormick's biographer, William T. Hutchinson; assisted Cyrus Bentley in preparing his unpublished refutation of the claim made by members of the Leander J. McCormick family that Robert McCormick II was the inventor of the reaper rather than his son, Cyrus Hall McCormick; and made progress reports to the McCormick family.

In 1951, when Anita McCormick Blaine, as the only surviving member of the Association presented all of its holdings to the State Historical Society of Wisconsin, Dr. and Mrs. Kellar continued as co-ordinators of the Collection at Madison until his death in 1955 and her retirement in 1963. These files then came to an end, and responsibility for the McCormick Collection was assumed by other staff members at the Society.

14. SPECIAL REPORTS FILE. PAPERS, 1893–1963.
    47 boxes.

A collection of research reports, speeches, biographical essays, term papers, masters' theses, and doctoral dissertations compiled and written by students, historians, and independent researchers. These are all related to the McCormick family and its companies, many of them being based on manuscripts in the McCormick Collection itself.

A card index to authors and titles accompanies the file.

COLLATERAL PAPERS

15. ADAMS, ROBERT MCCORMICK (1847–1925). PAPERS, 1869–1953. 5 boxes.

Correspondence, receipts, and reports of R. M. Adams, son of Cyrus Hall McCormick's sister, Amanda, including many letters from his wife and children; his brother, Edward S. Adams; and his sister-in-law, Grace C. (Mrs. James W.) Adams, and her sons. The papers, separated from the files of Nettie Fowler McCormick, Cyrus H. McCormick, Jr., and Anita McCormick Blaine, reflect many years of appeals by members of the Adams family for cash gifts and loans from the McCormicks due to financial reverses, medical costs, and the struggle to educate the Adams' children.

16. GEISER MANUFACTURING COMPANY. MINUTES, 1884–1898. 1 box including 3 volumes.

By-laws and minutes of the board, 1884–1898, of the Geiser Manufacturing Company, Waynesboro, Pennsylvania, manufacturer of grain thrashers; self-regulating grain separators, cleaners, and baggers; triple-geared horse powers for wagons; and other agricultural implements. Several clippings concerning the early personnel and history of the company, incorporated in 1869, are mounted in the volumes of minutes.

17. HOUGHTON, CHESTER (1835–1865). DIARY, 1858. 4 typewritten pages.

Extracts from the diary of a young Walworth County, Wisconsin, farmer in which references are made to his attempt to perfect a reaper at a shop in Palmyra, and his desire to interest John F. Appleby in the machine.

18. JACKSON AND CONWAY. CORRESPONDENCE, 1874–1875.
   1 volume.

Letterpress copy book of a firm operated by W. M. Jackson and M. R. Conway, Columbus, Ohio, wholesale and retail dealers in agricultural implements, containing letters concerning debts, deliveries, orders, and shipments.

19. KELLAR, HERBERT ANTHONY (1887–1955). PAPERS, 1600–1961.
   201 boxes including 5 volumes.

Papers of Herbert A. Kellar, curator for the McCormick Historical Association from 1915 to 1955, consisting of personal and professional correspondence; speeches. research notes and bibliographies relating to Cyrus Hall McCormick, genealogy, the reaper, patent cases, and agriculture; correspondence and other materials documenting Kellar's active membership in professional organizations; and the papers of Solon Robinson, agricultural journalist, and Everett E. Edwards, agricultural historian. Kellar's own investigations concerning the invention and development of the reaper, the papers of Robinson, and research notes collected by Edwards account for most manuscripts prior to 1900 and comprise about one-half the total quantity of papers.

As curator for the McCormick Collection, Kellar corresponded with numerous persons, particularly the historian of the South Ulrich B. Phillips, in his search for collateral papers relating to the McCormicks, the growth of industry, and the history of agriculture; gathered information preparatory to his supervision of the restorations at "Walnut Grove," the McCormick ancestral home in Virginia; made reports on the progress of the McCormick Historical Association; and in 1923 completed a three-volume manuscript called "The Life and Times of Mr. C. H. McCormick, 1835–1844" (unpublished).

As a trained historian, Herbert Kellar became associated with many projects, organizations, and libraries interested in preserving historical records. He regularly corresponded with historians, archivists, librarians, and agriculturists, accumulating extensive files of letters, minutes, committee reports, plans, and programs. A large portion of the papers demonstrates his work with these organizations, particularly with the Agricultural History Society of which he was president from 1922 to 1924; the American Association for State and Local History and its council; the American Council of Learned Societies and its unsuccessful plan to assist foreign depositories during World War II by microfilming records to bring to the United States for safekeeping; the American Historical Association and especially its committee on historical source materials; the national advisory committee of the Historical Records Survey under the Works Progress Administration, for which he was chairman of the national committee and adviser to the Illinois survey; and the Mississippi Valley Historical Association, of which he was a member of the policy committee and president in 1946 and 1947 respectively.

As a collector, Kellar not only acquired documents and manuscripts for the McCormick Collection, but also accumulated materials in which he was himself professionally interested, especially those concerning Robinson and Edwards. The twelve boxes of manuscripts relating to Solon Robinson, agricultural editor for Horace Greeley's *New York Tribune,* were obtained for the preparation of *Solon Robinson: Pioneer and Agriculturist* (1936), two volumes compiled and edited by Kellar. The seventy-six boxes of Everett E. Edwards papers given to Kellar contain Edwards' correspondence and articles as senior agricultural historian for the United States Department of Agriculture, 1920–1945; his personal letters and those written as editor of the department's publication, *Agricultural History;* and typewritten notes used by Lewis Cecil Gray in writing Gray's two-volume *History of Agriculture in the Southern States to 1860* (1941).

Organization of the Papers

The Herbert A. Kellar papers are organized in three parts. Kellar's own papers, 1821–1961, arranged according to subject and chronologically within each category, are grouped as to personal papers, his work for the McCormicks, and his organizational activities. The Solon Robinson papers, 1600–1939, dealing with Robinson, his notes, and his writings, are filed in chronological order by years. The Everett E. Edward papers are organized in three series: series one, 1920–1945, filed by years, contains his correspondence as historian for his department; series two, *ca.* 1928–1953, filed alphabetically by correspondent, includes personal and business communications; and series three, *ca.* 1837–1864, consists of research materials used by Lewis Cecil Gray, arranged in part by periods in the development of southern agriculture and in part by subject.

20. MARSH, CHARLES W. (1834–1918). CORRESPONDENCE, 1866–1900. Photostats of 25 items.

Correspondence of C. W. Marsh, who, with his brother William W. Marsh, operated the Marsh Harvester Manufacturing Company, first at Shabbana, Illinois, and later at De Kalb. This includes communications with other manufacturers such as William Deering, J. D. Easter, Emerson & Co., and Gammon & Deering concerning improvements, patents, and sales; letters exchanged with John F. Steward of the Deering Harvester Company relating to Steward's projected history of harvesting machines; and a description of one of the early Marsh harvesters.

21. PHILADELPHIA SOCIETY FOR PROMOTING AGRICULTURE. PAPERS, 1692–1892, 1936–1937. 1 box.

Selections from the papers of the Philadelphia Society for Promoting Agriculture, organized in 1785, consisting of manuscripts held by the society dated 1692 and 1717–1892, relating to agriculture and to agricultural implements and machinery; and correspondence, 1936–1937, of John M. Okie, assistant secretary, with Herbert A. Kellar concerning the acquisition of additional documents obtained by Okie and the society.

THE VIRGINIA PAPERS

THE FOLLOWING PAPERS, relating in time and place to Cyrus Hall McCormick's early life and continuing interest in Virginia, provide a background of social, business, economic, political, and agricultural conditions in his native state, especially in the Valley of Virginia. Family surnames familiar to the McCormicks appear and reappear in these Virginia papers, and references to the inventor and his family occasionally are found.

22. ANTHONY, ABNER A. (*ca.* 1798–1884). PAPERS, 1782–1899. 3 boxes including 1 volume.

Papers of a Bedford County, Virginia, minister, farmer and merchant, consisting of yearly tax receipts, Anthony's accounts with suppliers showing prices of general merchandise and drugs, charges by blacksmiths, detailed cost of building a gristmill in 1820, tobacco sales from his farm, county court settlements of debts, and an indenture of 1867 dividing Anthony's property. One volume contains his store accounts for 1821 to 1823; marriages performed by Anthony in the Virginia counties of Bedford, Campbell, Franklin, and Pittsylvania, 1829–1836 and 1841–1863; and a list of male residents in his district.

23. ARMENTROUT, GEORGE W. (1848–1923). PAPERS, 1832–1922. 4 boxes including 12 volumes.

Papers of an Augusta County, Virginia, lawyer, farmer, and businessman, consisting of scattered correspondence concerning land and lumber interests and his law practice; personal accounts for purchases of household supplies and drygoods; and financial records, 1881–1892, of the firm of Hanger (Jacob A.) and Armentrout, dealers in agricultural implements, sawmill equipment, and leather belting at Staunton, Virginia. Also included are legal papers and genealogical notes used in Armentrout's search for the heirs of Scarlet Daugherty.

24. BACON AND LEWIS. RECORDS, 1805–1871.
    3 boxes including 11 volumes, and 6 volumes.

Financial records of a general merchandise firm operated by A. Sidney Bacon and William Cook Lewis at Lexington, Virginia, mainly in the 1850's. These consist of daybooks and general accounts of the company, with occasional entries for A. S. Bacon & Co.; records of merchandise used for a time by the partners for their Washington Hotel; references to loans from James D. Davidson; and transfers from Bacon and Jordan to Bacon and Lewis. Included with the papers is one volume, 1852–1871, kept by Lewis as commissioner of the county court showing accounts and estate sales for residents of Rockbridge County.

25. BRADY, DANIEL C. E. JOURNALS, 1860–1865.
    1 box including 2 volumes.

Two home journals kept presumably by Daniel C. E. Brady, nephew of William Weaver, at Buffalo Forge in Rockbridge County, Virginia. These contain a planting schedule; daily entries of work assignments for slaves and hired hands, including farm tasks, hauling of coal for the forge, and work at the shop; occasional mention of visitors to the Brady home including the McCormicks; a record of a diphtheria epidemic among the slaves in 1862; and a price list for equipment from Merchant Mill.

26. CENTRAL FARMER'S CLUB. MINUTES, 1873–1874.
    1 volume.

Minutes of almost monthly meetings, February 7, 1873, to September 24, 1874, of the Central Farmer's Club in Rockbridge

County, Virginia, including names of members and guests, and discussion topics relating to crops, farm management, and agriculture in the community.

27. CLAYTOR, ROBERT B. PAPERS, 1844–1891.
1 box.

Papers of a drygoods and clothing merchant at Liberty, Virginia, consisting of correspondence of various members of the Claytor family, with frequent mention of relatives and events in Bedford County and references to Liberty's great fire of October 12, 1884; including particularly letters exchanged between the parents and their daughter, Evelyn, when the latter was attending Mount Vernon Institute in Baltimore, Maryland, 1884–1886. The papers also contain letters from both Claytor and his father-in-law, Alfred A. Bell, when each made buying trips to eastern cities.

28. COLEMAN, LINDSEY. PAPERS, 1777–1873.
2 boxes.

Papers of a planter and merchant in Augusta County, Virginia, consisting of miscellaneous receipts; promissory notes; indentures; blacksmith charges; purchases of general merchandise for various members of the family, especially Coleman himself, his brother William, and his son Joseph; and an account, 1831, for auction of the estate of his mother, Judith [Coleman?] Tucker.

29. DAVIDSON, JAMES DORMAN (1808–1882). PAPERS, 1805–1885.
73 boxes including 36 volumes, and 14 volumes.

Papers of James D. Davidson, a lawyer of Lexington, Virginia, including correspondence, personal financial records, legal accounts, travel diaries, and memoranda concerning his court cases. Included are correspondence and records associated with his immediate family, especially two of his sons who practiced with their father until Greenlee was killed at Chancellorsville in 1863

and Charles A. died in 1879; and ledgers of Dorman and Davidson, kept by Davidson and his cousin, Charles P. Dorman, while
they were partners, 1832–1841.

As a busy county-seat lawyer, Davidson dealt with a wide
variety of matters, giving assistance to local businessmen and
ironmasters; representing clients in civil suits, collection of debts,
rental of slaves, and sale of lands; administering amnesty oaths
and purchasing supplies for the Home Guard during the Civil
War; and assisting soldiers in securing paroles and claiming
pensions. Correspondence is concerned in large part with his
legal work in the settlement of estates, including those of many
families whose names were well known in the area: Armentrout,
Caruthers, Estill, Frazier, Glasgow, Greenlee, Grigsby, Hamilton,
Houston, Jordan, Luckess, McChesney, McClung, McCorkle,
McCormick, McDowell, McNutt, Moore, Paine, Patton, Paxton,
Poague, Preston, Shields, Trevey, Willson, and Wilson. To a
much lesser extent the correspondence, receipts, and memoranda
reflect his interest in public works, land speculation, and education. References are found to the James River and Kanawha
Company; the North River Navigation Company; the Howardsville and Rockfish Turnpike Company; lands in Alabama,
Mississippi, and Missouri; and Washington College and its successor, Washington and Lee University, of which he was a
trustee. In addition, letters often contain observations on social
affairs and politics.

As an old-line Whig, Davidson's interest and influence in
politics account for many letters relating to slavery, the approach-
ing clouds of war, Virginia's secession convention of 1861, the
conduct of the war, and reactions to the Confederate government. For example, he corresponded with Samuel McDowell
Moore and Charles P. Dorman, state legislators; with congressman and later wartime governor John Letcher; with Alexander
H. H. Stuart, congressman, senator, and Secretary of the Interior
under President Fillmore; and with old Whig friends such as
Daniel D. Waite. Other correspondents among clients, lawyers,
educators, and friends include Hugh Adams, William W. Boyd,

J. B. Breckinridge, John W. Brockenbrough, Boliver Christian, James B. Dorman, E. N. Davis, John Echols, John T. Finley, William Frazier, William P. Greenlee, Thomas D. Houston, John D. Imboden, John W. and Samuel Francis Jordan, W. C. Lewis, C. H. Locher, James McChesney, James McDowell the son of former governor James McDowell, Jr., Henry A. McCormick, Thomas J. Michie, John J. and R. B. Moorman, James H. Paxton, John T. and Thomas L. Preston, John F. Shields, William H. Taylor, William Weaver, and Lewis Webb.

Davidson's personal life is revealed in communications from relatives, his account of a trip to Europe in 1851 and Greenlee's diary of a journey to Chicago and the Northwest in 1857, his political essays written under the pseudonym Robert of Rockbridge, and his financial records. Descriptions of army life appear in letters from his sons, only one of whom, Charles A., survived the period of the Civil War, to become commissioner in chancery at Lexington. In contrast to letters from his brother in Virginia, Henry G. Davidson, those from his other brothers in Indiana, Alexander H. and Charles B. Davidson, reveal reactions of Virginians in the North as war affected the nation. The correspondence also contains the original General Order No. 43 respecting paroles for the Army of Northern Virginia agreed upon by Grant and Lee at Appomattox, April 11, 1865.

Organization of the Papers

The James D. Davidson papers are organized in two series. Series one, 1805–1885, containing Davidson's own papers, accounts for more than 95 per cent of the material. Series two, 1856–1880, contains correspondence and record books of Charles A. Davidson.

30. GRAVES, WILLIAM. PAPERS, 1831–1879.
     1 box.

Papers of a merchant who operated general merchandise stores, first at Mechum's River in Albemarle County, Virginia, and then at Liberty in Bedford County, consisting of correspondence, receipts, and agreements relating to William Graves's stores and collection agency; letters from his sons while they were attending Washington College in Lexington, 1866–1871; one letter written on behalf of Robert E. Lee regarding room and board at the College; and accounts for a store owned by Dennis Nalley (d. 1840) in Nelson County, whose estate Graves administered.

31. HARRIS, HENRY ST. GEORGE. PAPERS, 1840–1914.
1 box.

Papers of a planter at Bolling's Landing, Buckingham County, Virginia, consisting of letters exchanged with members of the Harris family and their friends, including especially correspondence with the Thomas F. Nelson family.

32. HENRICO COUNTY, VIRGINIA. ACCOUNT BOOKS, 1810–1812.
2 volumes.

Records for Henrico County, Virginia, kept by tax collectors James Bailey and John McMorris, recording the amount of property tax each resident in the district paid for land, Negroes, and horses. Indexed.

33. HOUSTON, WILLIAM H. (1787–1868). PAPERS, 1824–1868.
1 folder.

Papers of a farmer in Rockbridge County, Virginia, consisting of copies of diaries recording yearly harvesting activities, many comments on politics, and the price of commodities during the Civil War; including also an inventory of William H. Houston's estate at the time of his death, and an inventory of the estate of Thomas Willson, who died in 1858.

34. JONES, HENRY B. PAPERS, 1831–1882.
2 folders including 2 volumes, and 1 volume.

Papers of a farmer and merchant of Rockbridge County, Virginia, containing some correspondence but chiefly scattered receipts; one ledger for his Lexington store; and two account books in which he recorded carpentering and hauling for others, his own farm and family expenses, and yields from an apple orchard and his selection of trees. Included are typewritten notes taken from a diary kept by Jones, 1842–1847, relating to members of the McCormick family.

35. JORDAN AND DAVIS. PAPERS, 1831–1897.
   5 boxes.

Papers of Samuel Francis Jordan (1805–1872) and his brother-in-law, William W. Davis, ironmasters, merchants, and millers, covering chiefly the period when they operated as partners, *ca.* 1833–1853, at Jane Furnace and Gibraltar Forge in Rockbridge County, Virginia. These consist of correspondence, accounts relating to orders for iron and purchases of supplies and equipment, promissory notes, indentures, and agreements to hire slaves for labor. A few items refer to Jordan's operation of the Buena Vista Furnace, purchased in 1848. Evidence of trade in kind and cash sales involving other ironmasters and merchants is common, including particularly trade with W. M. Bryan at Vesuvius Furnace, James S. Dickinson at Bath Forge, John W. Jordan at California Furnace, William H. Jordan at Buena Vista Furnace, William Weaver at Buffalo Forge, Compton and Taylor, McDaniel and McCorkle, Montgomery and Irvine, and James M. Webb & Co.

After dissolution of the partnership an inventory of Gibraltar Forge was made, and the papers then become those of Davis, whose son, James C. Davis, was his partner for a time. Five letters appear from the latter, 1862–1865, while he was a Confederate soldier. Included also are letters from Baptist ministers such as J. William Jones, and letters from W. A. Kuper and Mathew Pilson regarding the Howardsville and Rockfish Turnpike Company, of which Davis was a director.

A card catalog accompanies the papers.

36. JORDAN AND IRVINE. PAPERS, 1803–1871.
7 boxes including 14 volumes.

Business papers of John W. Jordan (1777–1854) and John Irvine (b. 1781) of Rockbridge County, Virginia, ironmasters, builders, merchants, and millers, representing their activities both before and after they formed their partnership in 1821. Although there are many accounts for the purchase and sale of general merchandise, most of the papers concern the company's construction of a canal for the James River and Kanawha Company, production of iron at furnaces and forges in Rockbridge County, and plans for the Bath Iron Works in Alleghany County. Papers of 1823 to 1826 include specifications, estimates, registers of workmen, and letters pertaining to procurement of supplies and slave labor for building the canal around Balcony Falls. After 1826, the manufacture and sale of iron account for most of the correspondence and records.

The papers contain communications with local planters and merchants such as Robert Brooks, John F. Caruthers, William H. Graves, James McDowell, Jr. (1795–1851), who became governor, John Ruff, and William Willson; with business agents and dealers in Lynchburg and Richmond such as Samuel McCorkle, Bernard Peyton, Robert White, and Lewis Webb & Co.; and with ironmasters such as William Lusk, William Weaver, and Jordan's son, Samuel Francis Jordan. Included also are letters and receipts from lawyer James D. Davidson and county clerk Samuel McDowell Reid; one volume showing property tax levies and collections for residents of Rockbridge County in 1806; and an iron forge account book, 1843–1844, kept by Joseph Y. Trevey and Washington Jackson.

A card catalog accompanies the papers.

37. McCORMICK, NATHANIEL DAVIS (b. 1826–[?]). ACCOUNT BOOKS, 1852–1905. 2 volumes.

Record books kept by Nathaniel Davis McCormick and his

brother, Robert Alexander McCormick (1831–1862), second cousins of Cyrus Hall McCormick, documenting a half century of gristmill and farm activity in Rockbridge and Augusta counties in Virginia. These include accounts for grinding grains at McCormick's Mill; farm expenses, crop production, threshing costs, and pasturing; horse breeding in 1885; and sales from a general merchandise store.

38. McCORMICK, STEPHEN (1784–1875). PAPERS, 1827–1838. 1 box including 3 volumes, and 1 package.

Papers of Stephen McCormick, Auburn, Virginia, inventor of a cast-iron plow, consisting of one account book, 1827–1838, recording plows sold and repaired, farm produce, and labor costs; two daybooks, 1832–1833 and 1838, for a general store, one probably operated by his son-in-law's father, J. W. Catlett, in which many entries appear for Stephen McCormick and his family; a patent, October 22, 1828, signed by John Quincy Adams; and specifications for improvements in McCormick's plow. Any relationship with Cyrus Hall McCormick's own family line would have been very distant.

39. McCORMICK, WILLIAM STEELE [STEEL] (1804–1883). PAPERS, 1833–1879. 1 box.

Papers of a cousin of Cyrus Hall McCormick who moved from Virginia to Missouri in 1840. Correspondence consists of early letters from relatives in Augusta and Montgomery counties in Virginia making frequent references to residents there, especially the family of his wife who had been Rebecca Crow, and mentioning the sale of their Virginia iron furnace and reapers by Robert McCormick II and by Cyrus Hall McCormick; and later letters relating to William Steele McCormick's agency for the sale of McCormick reapers in Missouri. The papers also contain a genealogy of the L. P. Rowland family of Missouri, into whose family a McCormick daughter married.

40. McDowell, James (1770–1835). Papers, 1739–1849.
12 boxes including 1 volume, and 2 volumes.

Papers of James McDowell, Rockbridge County, Virginia, planter and distiller, and father of James McDowell, Jr. (1795–1851), who was governor of Virginia from 1843 to 1846. These are composed of correspondence, indentures, promissory notes, charges for general merchandise and medical care, account books, and records of the 8th Regiment of Virginia Militia commanded by Col. McDowell. Land transfers and descriptions appear throughout, first concerning large acquisitions from the Borden Tract along the James River, and after 1800 concerning speculations of McDowell and his partner, Andrew Reid, in Ohio lands, and McDowell's own holdings in Kentucky. His years as justice of the peace account for the presence of numerous documents relating to small claims and estate settlements.

Although few of his own letters are present, he received many from friends. For instance, Congressman James Breckinridge kept him informed on national banking and foreign affairs both before and after the War of 1812; his agents in Ohio, Nathaniel Pope and W. A. Trimble, and his agent in Kentucky, Nathaniel Hart, wrote him of conditions in those states; and letters from John. H Peyton, Francis Preston, and John Preston discuss business and politics in Virginia. One letter from Hart, March 9, 1807, discusses the Aaron Burr expedition; and one dated January 24, 1822, from James McDowell, Jr., to Thomas Hart Benton comments on President Monroe's policies.

In addition, the papers contain a complete inventory of his estate, 1835, including the age and reputed value of each of his forty-one slaves; and an 1824 manuscript plat map of Pattonsburg, Virginia. In three volumes McDowell recorded sales of produce, livestock, and whiskey from his plantations; and the sale of internal revenue stamps, 1796–1801.

41. Merchant Account Books. Record Books, 1791–1889.
41 volumes.

An assortment of daybooks, ledgers, journals, and inventories kept by twenty-one different merchants in Rockbridge County, Virginia, most of them relating to the operation of general merchandise stores at Lexington, showing prices of commodities and purchases by county residents. Chief among the merchants and firms represented are John F. Caruthers, Caruthers and Patton, Caruthers and Shields, James Compton, H. M. Estill, William Finley, William McDaniel, Jr., John Patton, Willson and Patton, James R. Willson, Samuel Willson, and William Willson.

42. JOHN H. MYERS & SON. RECORD BOOK, 1860–1866.
    1 volume.

Daybook used by John H. Myers & Son of Lexington, Virginia, in which are recorded charges made for blacksmithing, including small iron manufacturing and repair work.

43. REID, SAMUEL McDOWELL (1790–1869). PAPERS, 1783–1867.
    1 box including 4 volumes, and 3 volumes.

Papers of Samuel McDowell Reid, a planter of Lexington, Virginia, who succeeded his father, Andrew Reid, as clerk of the Rockbridge County court, consisting of receipts and promissory notes, accounts for his plantation and mill and for estates of which he was executor, charges made to him for blacksmithing and iron repairs, and stock certificates and reports for the James River and Kanawha Company. Also included are personal account books of his father and his father-in-law, William B. Hare of Lynchburg; and financial records, 1808–1818, for Ann Smith Academy at Lexington.
    A card catalog accompanies the papers.

44. ROBINSON, JOHN (1753–1826). PAPERS, 1810–1837.
    1 box including 3 volumes.

Papers of a wealthy unmarried planter and whiskey distiller in

Rockbridge County, Virginia, containing limited correspondence, receipts, agreements, orders for sales of liquor, purchases at a general store, his will, an inventory of his estate sold at his "Hart's Bottom Plantation" in 1826, and accounts for the hire and sale of Negro slaves inherited from Robinson by Washington College at Lexington.

45. ROCKBRIDGE COUNTY AGRICULTURAL SOCIETY. PAPERS, 1827–1857. 1 folder including 1 volume.

Record book of the Rockbridge County Agricultural Society in Virginia consisting of one volume containing constitution, minutes, and members, 1827–1838; and additional lists of members showing dues paid, 1853–1857.

46. ROWAN, JAMES (1800–1876). PAPERS, 1774–1870. 1 box including 10 volumes, and 1 volume.

Records of an Augusta County, Virginia, farmer consisting of receipts and ledgers for his plantation and accounts for a general store. The papers also contain receipts and ledgers for a tanning business operated by his father, James Rowan (who originally spelled the name Roan), showing purchases of hides and skins during and following the American Revolution; an unidentified blacksmith's daybook, 1793–1794; and three manuscript ciphering books, 1803–1806.

47. SMILEY, WILLIAM (ca. 1800–1879). PAPERS, 1860–1867. Typewritten copies of 13 items.

Letters and accounts of a farmer in Augusta County, Virginia, chiefly concerning his care of a soldier during the Civil War; including also one letter, January 17, 1865, from a minister describing conditions at Confederate camps near Richmond and at Libby Prison.

48. STERRETT, WILLIAM M. PAPERS, 1857–1885.
    1 folder including 3 volumes.

Farm accounts, wages paid, receipts, and general merchandise
purchased and sold by a landowner and merchant in Rockbridge
County, Virginia; including cattle sales and an agreement for
renting to a tenant farmer.
A card catalog accompanies the papers.

49. TYE RIVER AND BLUE RIDGE TURNPIKE COMPANY. PAPERS,
    1829–1843. 1 folder including 1 volume.

Treasurer's book, 1829–1843, kept by William Massie of Rockbridge County, Virginia, for the Tye River and Blue Ridge
Turnpike Company, including lists of subscribers for construction of the road; and letters to Massie, 1842, from both Robert
McCormick II and his son, Cyrus Hall McCormick, making arrangements for their payments to the company.

50. TYE RIVER WAREHOUSE. ACCOUNTS, 1826–1866.
    2 boxes including 17 volumes.

Records for a warehouse operated by Frederick Mortimer Cabell
at the confluence of the Tye and James rivers in Nelson County,
Virginia. These consist of unbound volumes and loose pages of
daybooks, ledgers, debt summaries, storage records, and inventories. Two of the account books, 1830–1831 and 1835–1840,
record shipments for tobacco planters in Rockbridge County,
the carrier, and the destination. The papers also contain an
agreement in 1838 for providing labor on the canal.

51. WALKER, JOHN. ACCOUNT BOOK, 1788–1795.
    1 volume.

Daybook kept by a Rockbridge County, Virginia, blacksmith,
consisting of his charges for blacksmithing and iron repair work
at his shop.

NON-MANUSCRIPT
MATERIALS

52. LIBRARY, MUSEUM, AND ICONOGRAPHIC ITEMS.

NO GUIDE TO THE manuscripts in the McCormick Collection can be complete without recognizing the vast amount of non-manuscript materials also presented to the State Historical Society of Wisconsin when the manuscripts were received. These are of many kinds—books, pamphlets, periodicals, broadsides, posters, photographs, portraits, farm machinery and models, mementoes, household items, and personal effects—covering in varying numbers the wide range of interests of members of the McCormick family.

In the *Library* about 2,000 books from the McCormick Collection fell within the scope of the Society's acquisition policies and have been cataloged. These are concerned with American history; the history of Virginia; the history of Chicago and guides for that city; agricultural history; the McCormick Theological Seminary; the Moody Bible Institute; the Young Men's Christian Association; philanthropy; trade publications as related to railroads, steam engines, and agriculture; almanacs; biographies; and McCormick family genealogies.

Several hundred pamphlets include reports and charters relating to the McCormick business interests, biographical sketches, local histories for Virginia and Chicago, and printed addresses bearing on topics in American history. Periodicals deal chiefly with American agriculture, the Presbyterian church, and state history, including especially *International Harvester World* (Chicago), from 1909 to the present (with the exception of 1913,

1915, 1949–1952, and 1963–1965); *New England Farmer* (Boston), 1852–1863; *Michigan Farmer* (Detroit), 1848–1855; *Farmer and Mechanic* (New York City), 1847–1852; *General Farmer* (Rochester, New York), 1842–1860; *The Interior* (Chicago), 1870–1891; and single issues of newspapers such as the *Richmond Republican,* 1849, 1851, and the Staunton *Valley Virginian,* 1891.

Museum items from the McCormick Collection are located in two places: in the Society's museum at Madison, and in its farm and craft museum at Stonefield, near Cassville, Wisconsin. In the Madison museum are well over a hundred numismatic items, many of them medals won by McCormick entries at international expositions or struck to commemorate events in the development of the reaper; more than one hundred items of clothing and personal effects, and eight household items, all from the period 1870 to 1920; and a few flags, machinery models, portraits, and pieces of sculpture.

By far the largest number of early agricultural machines from the McCormicks, and especially from the International Harvester Company, are located at Stonefield. These include full-size and/or scale models of binders, broadcast machines, choppers, corn planters, grain drills, hand cultivators, hay mowers, hay stackers, plows, rakes, reapers, rollers, and seeding machines. Models of the first reaper of 1831, an early Russian harrow, and a wooden fanning mill are also among the items. In addition, several pieces relating to early farm life are included: a cathedral heating stove, butter churns, sewing machines, a butter-print machine, and an ox cart.

Iconographic materials are many and varied. These include hundreds of photographs of the McCormicks, their relatives, and friends; officials of their companies; and places and organizations in which they were particularly interested, such as the McCormick Theological Seminary, schools and missions to which they contributed, and buildings in Chicago. Architectural drawings, some by Louis H. Sullivan, concern McCormick residences and McCormick-financed buildings for institutions; and surveys and photographs show changes at the "Walnut Grove" property in Virginia. Maps and plats include a few foreign cities and countries visited by the family, but are related chiefly to Chicago, the Lake Forest development, and Cook County, Illinois.

Lithographs, photographs, posters, and broadsides document the development of the reaper and the growth of both the McCormick Harvesting Machine Company and the International Harvester Company, including pictures of many of their agencies and their exhibits at international exhibitions. Advertising circulars, distributed almost annually between about 1853 and 1878, are included, as are photographs on methods of harvesting; glass plates of harvesting activities of early competitors; and a film, *The Romance of the Reaper,* made for the 1931 centennial celebration.

Most of the books, museum items, and maps are catalogued; many family photographs, albums, and company circulars are filed; but a great number of iconographic items are as yet unprocessed for research use.

APPENDIX

Robert McCormick II *m.* Mary Ann Hall, 1808
   Cyrus Hall[1] *m.* Nancy Maria (Nettie) Fowler, 1858
   Robert Hall *d.* at age sixteen
   Susan Jane *d.* at age twelve
   William Sanderson *m.* Mary Ann Grigsby, 1848
   Mary Caroline *m.* James Shields, 1847
   Leander James *m.* Henrietta Hamilton, 1845
   John Prestly *d.* at age twenty-nine
   Amanda Joanna *m.* Hugh Adams, 1845

Cyrus Hall McCormick—Nettie Fowler McCormick
   Cyrus H., Jr.[2] *m.* Harriet B. Hammond, 1889
     Cyrus Hall *m.* Dorothy Linn, 1915
     ————— *m.* Florence Davey, 1931
     Elizabeth *d.* at age twelve
     Gordon[3]
     ————— *m.* Alice Marie Hoit, 1927
     Mary Virginia[3]
     Robert *d.* at age two
   Anita *m.* Emmons Blaine, 1889
     Emmons, Jr. *m.* Eleanor Gooding, 1917
       Anne (Nancy) *m.* Gilbert Harrison, 1951

---

[1]Commonly signed his name as C. H. McCormick.

[2]Originally named Cyrus Rice, in his youth changed to Cyrus Hall, and for many years thereafter signed his name as Cyrus H. McCormick, Jr.

[3]Never married.

Alice *d.* at age one
Harold Fowler *m.* Edith Rockefeller, 1895
    John Rockefeller *d.* at age four
    Harold Fowler[4] *m.* Anna Stillman, 1931
    Muriel *m.* Elisha Dyer Hubbard, 1931
    Editha *d.* at age nine months
    Mathilda *m.* Max Oser, 1923
        Anita
        Peter Max
    —————— *m.* Ganna Walska, 1922
    —————— *m.* Adah Wilson, 1938
Stanley Robert *m.* Katherine Dexter, 1904

[4]Familiarly known as Fowler.

INDEX

All numerals refer to entry numbers, not to pages.
Italicized numerals indicate individual collections.

Christian, Bolivar, 1, 29
Christian education, 2
Christiansen, Emil, 5
Cimarron Ranch, New Mexico, 7
Cincinnati, Ohio, 1
Civil War, 2, 47
Clark, Preston, B. 3
Clarke, John H., 5
Claytor, Evelyn, 27
Claytor, Robert B., 27
Clemenceau, Georges, 3
Clemens, William C., 2
Clemons, Harold S., 2
Clough, Edwin M., 5
Cobb, D. W., 8
Coile, S. A., 2
Colahan, Charles, 1, 2
Colby, Everett, 5
Coleman, Joseph, 28
Coleman, Lindsey, 28
Coleman, William, 28
College of the Ozarks, Arkansas, 2
Columbia Theological Seminary, South Carolina, 2
Committee of Fifteen, 5
Committee to Defend America by Aiding the Allies, 5
Commodity prices, 33
Compton, James, 41
Compton and Taylor, 35
Confederate camps, 47
Confederate government, 29
Conger, Arthur L., 11
Conkling, Roscoe, 1
Consolidated Implement Company, 8
Constant, Paul d'Estournelles de, 3
The Continent, 2, 3
Conway, M. R., 18
Cook County, Illinois, 52; Normal School, 5
Cooke, Flora J., 5
Copeland, C. C., 1, 3
Cory, Harlan Page, 2
Cothran, James S., 1
Cothran, James S., Jr., 1, 2, 3
Cotopaxi furnace, 1
Couchman, W. V., 3, 7, 8

Council Bluffs, Iowa, 6
Cox, James M., 5
Craig, Willis G., 1, 2, 3
Crane, Charles R., 6
Cranston, Ruth, 5
Cravath, Paul D., 3, 6
Crédit Foncier, 1
Crédit Mobilier, 1
Crone, R. B., 2
Crow family, 39
D. M. Osborne & Company, 8, 9
Damrosh, Margaret Blaine, 5
Daugherty, Scarlet, 23
Davidson, Alexander H., 29
Davidson, Charles A., 29
Davidson, Charles B., 29
Davidson, Greenlee, 29
Davidson, Henry G., 29
Davidson, James Dorman, 29, 1, 24, 36
Davies, Joseph E., 5
Davis, E. N., 29
Davis, Edward P., 3
Davis, James C., 35
Davis, William W., 35
Dawes, Charles G., 3, 6
Day, George M., 2
Day, Henry, 1, 2
Day, Mrs. Henry, 2
Dealers' catalogs, 8, 9
de Bey, Cornelia B., 5
de Constant, Paul d'Estournelles, 3
de Madariaga, Salvador, 5
Deepwater Coal and Iron Corporation, 3
Deering, Charles, 2, 3
Deering, James, 2, 3, 7
Deering, William, 1, 2, 11, 20
Deering Harvester Company, 3, 9, 20
Deering twine mill, 9
De Kalb, Illinois, 20
Democratic Party, 3, 5, 6; membership in, 1
Democratic State Central Committee, Illinois, 1
Deschanel, Paul, 3
Dewey, George, 3

INDEX